COUNTRY
DOUGHCRAFT
DESIGNS

READER'S DIGEST

COUNTRY DOUGHCRAFT DESIGNS

55 Step-by-Step Projects

LINDA ROGERS

Reader's Digest

READER'S DIGEST ASSOCIATION INC.
Pleasantville, New York / Montreal

This book is dedicated to the memory of my
grandmother, Bertha Amelia Johnson, business-
woman and craftsperson, in whose footsteps
I would like to follow.

Page 2 Duck wall plaque (see page 111)

The designs featured in this book are available commercially
as finished items. Further information is available from
Dough Designs, The Old School, Gretton Road,
Gotherington, Cheltenham, Gloucestershire GL52 4EP, England.
It is an infringement of the law of copyright to copy these designs
for commercial purposes.

A READER'S DIGEST BOOK

Edited and produced by David & Charles
First published in the UK in 1994

Photography by Paul Biddle
Illustrations by Lorraine Harrison

Text and designs copyright © Linda Rogers, 1994
Photography copyright © David & Charles, 1994

Library of Congress Cataloging in Publication Data

Rogers, Linda.
    [55 country doughcraft designs]
    Country doughcraft designs : 55 step-by-step projects / Linda
Rogers.
        p.   cm.
    First published in Great Britain in 1994 under the title : 55
country doughcraft designs.
    Includes index.
    ISBN 0-89577-966-8
    1. Bread dough craft.   2. Decoration and ornament, Rustic.
3. Decoration and ornament—Plant forms.   4. Decoration and
ornament—Animal forms.   I. Title.
TT880.R64   1997
745.5—dc21   97-3329

CONTENTS

INTRODUCTION

A wonderful piece of old German folklore tells that a piece of *Salzteig*, or salt dough, was given to a bridal couple by the bride's mother as a good luck charm. Its simple ingredients of flour, salt, and water represented the essentials for sustaining life; thus the household would never starve. The practice still continues today, but the modern gift consists of a loaf of bread and a bag of salt.

Salt dough was popular all over eastern Europe in the early nineteenth century, and peasants used to make salt-dough Christmas-tree decorations, adding a high percentage of salt to deter rats from eating them.

My introduction to doughcraft was purely by chance. Four years ago, I was fascinated to see "A Demonstration of Salt Dough Sculpture" being advertised on the program of our local young wives' group. I duly went along to the meeting with very little idea of what to expect. Since that day, I have been totally addicted to dough sculpture – as has the rest of my family, fortunately.

Everybody has creative ability, and immense satisfaction can be gained from producing a beautiful sculpture. My enthusiasm for this medium grows almost daily, and I have obtained a great deal of pleasure from seeing other people's excitement as the projects grow before their eyes. Modeling dough is therapeutic and relaxing, as I have seen for myself in workshops for the elderly, the physically challenged, and children. Once you have mastered the basic techniques shown in the first chapter, you should find that the designs are all easy to assemble, and by varying, for example, the leaf type or flower used on a piece, you can bring a charming originality to your work.

Inspiration for designs can be drawn from a multitude of sources – household objects, nature, art, pictures, wood carvings, pottery, etc. Your only limits are the bounds of your imagination. The projects chosen for this book all reflect a rural theme, and a wide variety of subjects means that there is something suitable for everyone. I hope that these designs will inspire you to try your hand at doughcraft, and that you will enjoy your baking as much as I do.

Opposite Fruit Basket (page 60), Vase of Roses (page 92),
Thatched Cottage (page 100), and Mice and Porcupines (page 26)

1
GETTING
STARTED

THE DOUGH

*T*he basic ingredients for salt dough couldn't be simpler.

1 **Good-quality all-purpose flour** – poor-quality flour results in substandard dough texture.
2 **Fine-grain salt** – coarse sea salt produces a rough dough, which is harder to model.
3 **Water** – a smoother dough is achieved with room-temperature water, which helps to dissolve the grains of salt. However, make sure it is not too warm, or the gluten in the flour will develop, making the dough elastic and difficult to handle.

There are several optional extras:

Vegetable oil or glycerin – a tablespoon of either may be added with the water to the basic dough mix. They yield a slightly more pliable dough, but I find that the dough quickly forms a skin and does not develop that lovely golden-brown color associated with bread.

Wallpaper paste – a tablespoon of dry wallpaper paste can be added to the flour when you are making dough. It does not affect the consistency of the raw or cooked dough, and it has the advantage of containing a mold inhibitor.

Cornstarch or potato flour – a proportion of either may be substituted for the wheat flour. They do not contain the gluten that gives flour its elasticity, and therefore they produce a stronger, tougher dough. This is good for very fine, detailed work, but the dough is harder to work with and not really suitable for the projects in this book. The dough is also much whiter than that made from wheat flour, and even when it is baked, it has an uncooked appearance.

PAINTS

Water-based paints are the best and easiest to use and come in several forms: artists' watercolors, poster paint, acrylic, or gouache. They are all widely available from stationery stores as well as specialty art and craft stores.

Watercolors can be purchased in tubes or as small cakes. They yield a transparent color, so you will have to apply many layers to achieve an opaque finish. A gentle wash of color is effective, though, if you want to preserve the natural look of the dough.

Poster paint can be used on dough models, but the range of colors is more limited than water-color or gouache, so the coloring tends to be less subtle. The final texture may also be a bit powdery.

Acrylic paint dries to a hard, plasticlike finish, helping to protect the dough from moisture, but remember to wash your brush and palette well before the paint dries or they will be ruined. This quick-drying quality can also make blending of colors tricky.

Gouache paint is more opaque than watercolor, but it can be watered down to a delicate transparent wash. This makes it very versatile for use on salt-dough sculpture. Like watercolor, gouache is available in a wide choice of colors.

It is also possible to use solvent-based enamel paints. These can be expensive as quite a large amount is generally required. Since they are not water-based, they must be thinned with turpentine or mineral spirits.

VARNISH

A good-quality hard varnish is necessary to protect the finished dough sculpture. The best is clear polyurethane yacht varnish from a hardware store. There are numerous special varnishes available from craft stores, but they tend to be expensive and are often thin and watery, soaking into the dough rather than forming a protective waterproof coating.

TOOLS AND EQUIPMENT

*T*he tools and equipment for doughmaking are readily found in the kitchen, and very few special items are required. You will need:

Rolling pin
Mixing bowl
Sharp knife
Baking sheets and round cake pans – The salt in the dough will quickly attack the surface of the pans, causing them to rust. The nonstick variety are much hardier, but still not totally infallible. It is possible to cover the bottom with foil or paper, but these may stick and can prove expensive if you are making a lot of dough. If, however, you choose to do this, silicone baking parchment is the best. It is a good idea to set some old pans aside specifically for your dough, washing and drying them thoroughly after each use.

Modeling tools – All sorts of kitchen gadgets can be used for modeling and making patterns on the dough. No special tools are needed, but the most useful item is a thin wooden or bamboo skewer. A toothpick serves the same purpose, but it is not as strong, and the extra length makes the skewer easier to handle. Scissors, forks, knives, pastry wheel, icing crimpers and paper clips will also be useful.

Cutters – All shapes and sizes of cutters are useful, particularly leaf and flower shapes, although they are not absolutely necessary, since these shapes can be molded by hand.

Brushes – A pastry brush or wide paintbrush is necessary for wetting the dough while you are assembling your models. For painting, synthetic brushes are preferable to sable or bristle as they are much more durable, and both dough and acrylic paints are tough on brushes. A small round brush for fine work, a medium-sized one for general painting, and a ⅜-inch (10mm) flat brush for larger areas should be adequate. For varnishing, a 1½-inch (38mm) brush is most suitable, but make sure it is of good quality so your work doesn't end up covered in bristles.

Potato ricer or garlic press – These items are particularly useful as they make wonderful grass or hair by extruding long strands of dough through the holes. For the uninitiated, a potato ricer is like a giant garlic press and is widely used in the food service industry for mashing potatoes. Both tools are available from good kitchen departments or restaurant equipment suppliers, and also by mail order.

Cloves – Invaluable for stalks and eyes.

BASIC TECHNIQUES

MAKING DOUGH

It is best to use a measuring cup, although you could use a straight-sided mug to measure your ingredients. The basic ratio of ingredients is two of flour, one of salt, and one of water. For projects using smaller quantities of dough, you may prefer to measure the water in ounces and then divide or multiply this.

The table below, which gives the number of cups required of each ingredient, provides a quick reference – but *do* add the water carefully and sparingly to avoid making the mixture too wet.

A dough mixture using four cups of flour should be enough for a couple of large projects, such as a garland and basket, while a quantity of dough made with one cup of flour should be adequate to make a small model, such as a collection of mushrooms or a selection of small animals.

Sample Recipes for Dough

Flour	Salt	Water
4	2	2
3	$1\frac{1}{2}$	$1\frac{1}{2}$
2	1	1
1	$\frac{1}{2}$	$\frac{1}{2}$

Mix the flour and salt well, then add the water all at once and knead well. An electric mixer with a dough hook or beater is ideal for this, if yours is large enough. The most important part of making sculptures is to get the consistency of the dough right. It should be firm yet pliable, somewhere between the consistencies of bread dough and pie crust. A dough that is too dry will crumble and be difficult to work with; one that is too wet will be sticky to use and not hold its shape well. Different brands of flour absorb water to differing degrees, so

you may need to be a little flexible. It is always easy, however, to knead in a little more flour or add water to change the consistency of the dough. Note that a small difference in the amount of water added can change the consistency of the dough considerably, so add any extra sparingly. It may be enough just to wet your hands and re-knead the dough.

KNEADING

Once you have made your dough, it is important to knead it really thoroughly for at least five minutes. Although an electric mixer is useful for making the dough, it is always best to give it a final kneading by hand. The warmth of your hands helps to give the dough elasticity and to combine the grains of salt, yielding a smoother consistency.

STORING UNCOOKED DOUGH

I have read, and been told, that it is possible to store uncooked dough for some time, but I have never found this to be successful. Once the dough has been made up for more than a couple of hours, it is difficult to use. It attracts moisture from the atmosphere and becomes sticky. The gluten in the flour develops, making the dough more elastic. This reduces the sharpness of detail, as the dough does not hold its shape as well once molded.

If you do find it necessary to keep your dough, do not refrigerate it, but put it in a clean plastic bag. If it is left exposed to the air, it will form a dry skin. It is generally quicker and easier to make a fresh batch than to battle with inferior dough. Once it has been molded to the design, it should go straight into the oven. If the dough is left out, it will form a dry skin, which will crack once it is cooked.

MODELING DOUGH

If the dough is the proper consistency, it will be easy to work with. When rolling out dough, work with a floured rolling pin on a floured surface, and treat it exactly as you would pie crust.

When modeling by hand or rolling sausage shapes, it is best not to use flour. The dough will not stick to your hands and will be harder to shape if it is floured.

You will find that you need to wash your hands frequently while modeling, so work close to a sink. The kitchen obviously is an ideal workplace with a temperature that is usually suitable. If it is too cold, the dough will be stiff; if it is too warm, it may become too soft to work with.

It is best to work directly on your baking sheet, as moving your model once it is finished may distort it. Grease the tray very lightly with vegetable oil, or use baking parchment to line it.

JOINING DOUGH

When assembling your dough sculptures, dampen the relevant area slightly with a little water to join the component parts together. Too much water will produce a slippery, rather than a sticky, surface, and the pieces will tend to slide around.

Fresh dough can be used to join or repair ready-baked or hardened pieces of dough. Or, mix fresh dough with water to form a thick starch paste which can then be brushed onto the surfaces to be joined. Similarly, holes or cracks can be filled with fresh dough. When the seam is completed, if the piece has not been varnished, re-bake the dough on no more than 200°F (100°C) for an hour or so. This will be sufficient since only the small amount of fresh dough will need to cook. If the dough has been varnished, leave the seams to dry at room temperature.

If any pieces of dough need to be supported during baking, a crumpled piece of tinfoil placed underneath the piece will make a suitable prop. It can be removed once the dough is set.

USING TEMPLATES

Templates can provide shapes for doughcraft designs, allowing you to achieve just the outline you want and making it easier to repeat the shape.

Full-size templates have been provided for some of the projects in the book (see pages 118–26). To use, simply trace or photocopy the template onto thin cardboard. Cut out the shape, lay it lightly on top of the rolled out dough, and cut around the outline using a sharp knife.

The templates can also be used to enlarge or reduce designs. In this case, you will need to enlarge or reduce the template using a photocopier. Remember, of course, that dough requirements will also vary with the size and type of the model.

BAKING DOUGH

The oven temperature should be 200–250°F (100–120°C). As a rule of thumb, it takes approximately one hour for every ¼ inch (6mm) of dough thickness, but, as long as the temperature is no higher than 250°F (120°C), a longer period of time will do no harm. The drying-out process will take several hours.

Once you have experimented and become familiar with how long models take to cook in your own oven, you may find it convenient to bake overnight. The temperature of the oven can always be lowered slightly to compensate for the longer cooking time.

Once cooked, your dough should be golden-brown and should lift easily from the tray. Press it underneath at the thickest part and make sure it is not at all soft. A quick tap on the underside should produce a hollow sound. A dull sound will indicate that the dough in the center is still soft, so it should be returned to the oven. It is important that the dough be hard all the way through. If it is not, the model will continue to dry out after varnishing and will shrink and crack. All ovens are different, so experiment with moving dough around in your oven to achieve the best results.

PAINTING DOUGH

Make sure the dough sculpture is cold before you begin to paint, as the painted surface will become mottled if it is still hot. Water-based paints can be thinned with water to achieve different effects – thicker paints produce a bright, dramatic effect, while thinner paints are more subtle. The most successful results use water-based paints quite thinly, producing a slightly transparent effect, which is suitable for the projects in this book. A wide variety of colors are available in ready-to-use paints, but if you do not wish to buy many different colors, you can mix your own from the basic primary colors, using the color wheel below as a guide.

It is possible to color your dough before baking by using spices, food coloring, or powder paints. The particular projects that follow, however, are painted after they are baked.

If you want to leave your dough a natural color, it is possible to add emphasis to the detail by giving the piece a wash of thin red/brown paint all over, creating a sepia effect. Alternatively, you can use an egg wash to color your model. A deeper golden glaze is particularly effective on a bread ring or wheat sheaf. Simply beat an egg with a tablespoon of water and brush the mixture on the model before baking.

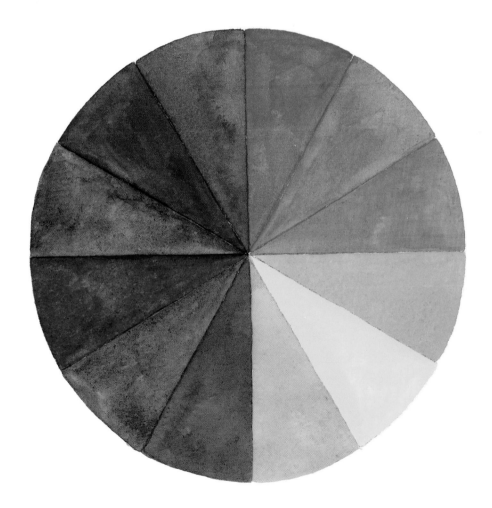

Basic Techniques

VARNISHING DOUGH

This is probably the most important part in the production of your sculpture, as it will succeed or fail on the quality of the varnishing.

It is imperative that the paint be completely dry before you begin or you will trap moisture in your model, which will cause the varnish to flake. Water-based paint does not take long to dry, and if it does not feel at all damp to the touch, you are ready to varnish. If in doubt, pop your model back into a cool oven or place it near a radiator for a few minutes.

When varnishing, make sure that every nook and cranny is well covered, as even a pinhead-sized hole in the varnish will trap moisture, which may soften the dough. Give your pieces at least two, but preferably three, coats of varnish on both sides for maximum protection. If you wear disposable gloves when varnishing, you need not be cautious about getting good coverage. Varnish your piece all over at once and leave it to dry on a wire rack for about six hours between coats. If you do not have a rack or something similar, you will need to varnish the back of the article first, and then, when that is dry, varnish the front, making sure that the varnish doesn't run through to the other side, causing drips and runs. Place the model on a plastic sheet to dry. It will lift off plastic easily, whereas paper will stick to the varnish.

CARE OF DOUGHCRAFT MODELS

Under normal household conditions, your dough should keep for many years. Kept in an excessively damp atmosphere, it may soften, but it can be re-hardened (see Troubleshooting). To clean it, simply dust or wipe with a damp cloth. After some time, you may find that a new coat of varnish will brighten it up. Do not place it in a steamy bathroom or near the stove; this may affect the varnish. Direct sunlight should be avoided, as it will fade the paint.

HANGERS

There are three basic ways to hang your sculpture on the wall.

HOLES
This method is suitable for small, fairly flat pieces of dough. Do not poke a hole in your piece with a skewer, since it may distort the shape and could close up in baking. It is better to cut out a piece using a strong plastic drinking straw as a miniature cutter.

RIBBONS
With a piece such as a basket, you can tie a ribbon around the handle, forming a loop with which to hang the model and a decorative bow. Thin ribbon can also be threaded through holes made in the dough.

HOOKS
A metal hook can be pushed into the raw dough and then baked in the model. As the dough cooks, it will swell slightly and mold itself around the hook, finally hardening and holding it in place. Hooks can be made from twisted pieces of florist's wire, hairpins or even loops of string, but by far the most convenient method is to use a suitably sized paper clip. Make absolutely sure it is large enough to penetrate well into the dough. Small paper clips are only suitable for the smallest projects; most will need at least a 1½-inch (38mm) long clip. The giant, wavy clips, available from stationery or office supply stores, are the most suitable for the larger projects. Try to make sure that when you push your hanger into your dough model, it will hang straight on the wall. This involves a certain amount of guesswork, but with a little practice you will soon be able to judge the center of gravity perfectly.

TROUBLESHOOTING

*H*aving mastered the basic techniques, you are all set to start creating your own beautiful models. If things should go wrong, don't despair – most problems are easily solved. The following is a list of the more common difficulties that may be encountered.

RISING, BLISTERING DOUGH

If the dough rises and forms bubbles during baking, this is an indication that either the dough was too wet or the oven too hot – or both. If the dough is still soft enough, pierce the bubbles with a pin and gently press back into shape. Reduce the temperature of the oven for the remainder of the cooking time. For future reference, if the dough is too soft, it will not hold its shape well and detail will be lost. If the oven is too hot, the dough will start to brown slightly before it hardens. This should help you decide what caused the problem and how to avoid it next time.

CRACKS

It seems that cracks that appear during or after baking are an occupational hazard. Although they are rare, sometimes it is almost impossible to avoid them. Cracks on the reverse of your model are incidental to the baking process and are not detrimental in any way to the piece. These are the sort of breaks that you find in bread. They appear more often in thicker models and can sometimes be avoided by cooking at a lower temperature.

The cracks that are particularly upsetting are the hairline cracks that appear after baking is complete. Changes of temperature cause slight expansion and contraction in the baked dough, causing stresses that can lead to cracking. Sometimes this happens during the cooling process, particularly with larger pieces, so it helps to cool them very slowly in the oven, gradually reducing the temperature until the oven is switched off. Leave the model in the oven until it is completely cool.

Another method that reduces the incidence of cracking, particularly in the larger pieces, is the same as that used for reinforcing concrete. Build up the base of your model in layers, inserting a piece of nylon net (available from any fabric store) between the layers. Full instructions for this are given in Chapter 7 on wall plaques.

If cracks appear after baking, they can be filled with a little fresh dough in the same way putty is used on plaster. If the model is already painted and varnished, leave the filler dough to dry out naturally in a warm room, then touch up with fresh paint and varnish. It is not advisable to rebake, as the changes in temperature may cause another crack.

SOFTENING DOUGH

If atmospheric conditions are exceptionally humid, or your dough models are kept in a very damp atmosphere, they may become soft and spongy. They can be rehardened by placing them on a radiator or in a warm place for several days. Alternatively, they may be placed in a cool oven (no more than 200°F (100°C) for 2–3 hours. This will darken the varnish slightly and will smell dreadful, but it will not harm your model in any way. If the varnish shows any sign of bubbling, it means that the oven is too hot.

REPAIRING BREAKAGES

Salt dough is fairly durable but will break if it is dropped. If the break is clean and your model is not broken in too many pieces, it can be repaired very successfully with Superglue or a resin-based adhesive which works with an added hardener.

If the damage is not extensive, such as an ear knocked off and lost or the end of a leaf crumbled away, the missing part of the model can be restructured using fresh dough. Let it dry in a warm place before retouching with paint and varnish.

FLAKING VARNISH

This condition is caused by dampness or steam. The appearance of your sculpture can be improved by rubbing away the flaking varnish with a rough cloth, such as terrycloth or, gently, with a very fine piece of emery paper, taking care not to scratch the paint underneath. Then give two coats of fresh varnish and rehang in a drier place.

*M*astering certain basic shapes, such as fruits, flowers, vegetables, leaves, breads, and so on, will allow you not only to produce the wide variety of designs in this book, but also to create your own original models.

Begin by rolling out the dough exactly as you would pie crust, using a floured rolling pin on a lightly floured surface. Flat shapes can be cut using cookie cutters or a sharp knife. If necessary, use a cardboard template by tracing the patterns at the back of the book (see pages 118–26). Other shapes are molded by hand.

FRUIT

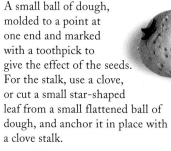

STRAWBERRIES
A small ball of dough, molded to a point at one end and marked with a toothpick to give the effect of the seeds. For the stalk, use a clove, or cut a small star-shaped leaf from a small flattened ball of dough, and anchor it in place with a clove stalk.

PEAR
A ball of dough, elongated and narrowed at one end, with a clove stalk, as in the apple, and a small leaf added.

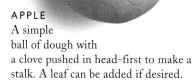

APPLE
A simple ball of dough with a clove pushed in head-first to make a stalk. A leaf can be added if desired.

GRAPES
Small balls of dough arranged in a slight S shape. Add leaf, stalk, and vine – a spaghetti-shaped piece of dough laid on top and twisted.

PLUMS
A small oval-shaped ball of dough, with a crease added down one side using a toothpick, and a hole pressed in the top. Size, shape, and color can be varied to produce cherries, peaches, apricots, etc.

ORANGE
A ball of dough "pitted" with the blunt end of a skewer, or rolled on the zesting part of a cheese grater to give the orange-peel effect. A clove with the seed broken off is used as the stalk.

BANANAS
Are best avoided!

FLOWERS

DAHLIA, MARIGOLD, CHRYSANTHEMUM
A stylized version of any of these can be made by placing a round ball of dough on top of a flattened piece and then snipping all the way around both pieces of dough with a small pair of scissors.

DAFFODIL
Assemble outer petals from flattened, elongated pieces of dough. The center is made from a small, sausage-shaped piece, flattened and then rolled up and placed on top of the outer petals.

PANSY
Five petals made from flattened balls of dough, slightly pointed at one end and assembled as shown in the photograph. Push a hole in the center with a skewer or toothpick.

DAISY SHAPE
This can be made from thinly rolled dough using a small sugarcraft cutter, or molded from a small, flattened ball of dough with the edges curled up with the tip of a toothpick. Push a hole in the center.

ROSE
The center of the rose is made from a flattened ball of dough rolled up to form a tight bud. The flower is built up to the required shape by overlapping successive flattened dough petals around the center bud.

LEAVES

USING CUTTERS
This method is especially useful for leaves of complicated shape, such as holly or ivy. Roll dough out thinly with a rolling pin and, after using the cutter, mark veins with a toothpick.

PINCHED LEAVES
A stylized leaf suitable for trees or hedges can be made by pinching a piece of dough between thumb and index finger, then breaking it off. Make a number, then pile them on top of each other.

CUTTING LEAVES FREEHAND
A simple leaf can be made from a rolled piece of dough by cutting it into long narrow strips and then cutting these into diamond shapes. Veins are marked with a toothpick.

MOLDED LEAVES
These can be made from a flattened ball of dough pinched to a point at one end. The sides can be drawn up with a skewer if desired to create more of an oak leaf effect. Mark veins as before.

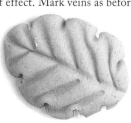

VEGETABLES

CAULIFLOWER

As for the cabbage below, but with a larger center ball and fewer outside leaves. Pit the center with the blunt end of a skewer, then, using the point or a toothpick, divide the cauliflower head into flowerets.

POTATO

Roll oval-shaped balls of dough and, using the blunt end of a wooden skewer, mark three or four eyes in each potato. They will look very realistic when painted.

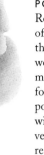

GREEN BEANS

Roll a long, thin piece of dough, thinnest at the very end, and flatten roughly, making indentations with your thumb at regular intervals.

LEEK

Flatten a long sausage of dough at one end, then cut off that end in a V shape. Add roots made from dough extruded through a garlic press and mark the leaves

TOMATOES

Make a small ball of dough, adding a star-shaped leaf held with a clove stalk as for a strawberry.

with a sharp knife. The best effect can be seen when painted.

CARROT

Roll a long, pointed piece of dough, and, then, using a very small circular cutter or the end of a cake decorating tip, mark a ring in the top of the carrot. Using a sharp knife, mark fine ridges across the carrot all the way down to its point.

MUSHROOMS

Roll a small ball of dough, and, using a very small circular cutter or the end of a cake decorating tip, press about halfway into the dough to form the stalk.

CABBAGE

Using a ball of dough for the center of the cabbage, build up the outside leaves in the same way as you add petals when making a rose.

ASPARAGUS

Roll a bundle of spear-shaped pieces of dough and snip the ends and shafts with nail scissors.

Roll a long piece of dough, flatten slightly, and mark the bark with a knife.

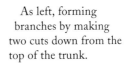

As left, forming branches by making two cuts down from the top of the trunk.

As right, but twisting two thinner versions together.

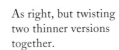

Roll a long sausage of dough, twist slightly, and pinch in places to create a gnarled appearance.

The base of a tree trunk needs to be finished off for a neat appearance. Either spread the base out slightly and add extruded dough as grass or plant it in a dough pot.

The possibilities here are endless, as you will realize if you have visited a good old-fashioned bakery. Poppy seeds, sesame seeds, rolled oats, and many other types of grains or seeds can be sprinkled on to add interest, but be sure to brush the top of your dough with water first or they won't stick. Bread rolls also make a good subject for refrigerator magnets. The following are a few examples of rolls that are easy to make.

FRENCH LOAF
A long, thin sausage of dough marked with diagonal cuts across the top.

ITALIAN BREAD
A shorter, fatter version of the French loaf.

COTTAGE LOAF
A small slightly flattened ball of dough placed on top of a larger one. Push a hole through the center and mark lines with a knife all around.

SESAME SEED BUNS
Traditional round burger buns.

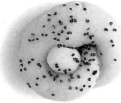

KNOT
Made from a long sausage of dough that is thinner at the ends and wrapped in a simple knot, this shape looks attractive when sprinkled with poppy seeds.

WHOLE WHEAT LOAF
This can be shaped from dough made with whole-wheat flour for texture and sprinkled with rolled oats.

PEASANT LOAF
A basic round loaf with a cross cut in the top.

BREAD AND ROLLS

BRAID WITH POPPY SEEDS

Traditional braid constructed from three sausage shapes, thinner at the ends. Your rolls of dough need to be twice as long as you require the finished braid to be.

SLICED LOAF

Form dough into a basic oblong shape, then using a sharp knife and a sawing motion, cut the slices from this fun loaf, leaving slices attached at the base so that they bend over as shown in the photograph.

PRETZEL

Made from a long roll of dough thinned out at each end.

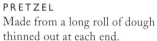

FEATHERS AND SPINES

Feathers can easily be marked on a wing-shaped piece of dough, using the end of a paper clip.

Snipping with scissors produces a featherlike effect (particularly suitable for owls). The cuts can be made in different sizes to create the effect of porcupine quills, flower petals, or sheaves of grain.

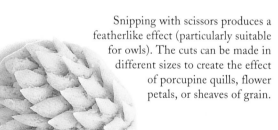

Extruded dough, pushed through a potato ricer or garlic press, makes wonderful hair. It can be cut off with a knife to different lengths to make grass, hair, sheep's wool, manes and tails, etc.

Wreaths are a very popular subject for salt-dough sculpture and can be formed in a variety of ways.

It is essential to keep your wreaths perfectly round; as any misshaping will spoil the effect. The best way to do this is to use a round baking sheet—for example, a pizza or an upturned cake pan—of approximately the size that you wish your finished wreath to be. By working directly onto this round pan and following its outline, you preserve the shape perfectly.

FLAT CUT-OUT WREATH

This can be made by rolling dough approximately ½ inch (13mm) thick and then choosing two round objects of suitable size, one slightly larger than the other – for example, a saucer and a salad plate. Place the larger plate on your dough and, using a sharp knife, cut around it. Then, making sure the smaller plate is centered, cut around that. This will result in a hollow, perfectly circular ring which can then be used as a base for your fruit, flowers, etc.

WREATH WITH LEAVES

Roll out a long snake of dough and place it around a circular pan, about an inch (25mm) from the edge, making sure that you leave enough space around the edge for the leaves. Press the two ends together to form a ring. Then make the leaves from flattened balls of dough following the instructions on page 17. Brush your ring with water (a paintbrush is the best tool for this), then simply place the leaves around the dough ring, pressing them gently into position.

TWISTED WREATH

This is made from two long rolls of dough. Before rolling your dough, give it an extra knead to ensure a good smooth finish. Roll out two snakes of dough approximately ¾ inch (19mm) thick and place them side by side. As a general guide their length should be three times the diameter of your baking pan.

With the two pieces side by side, roll them together in a twist, taking care to keep the twists even along the length of the dough. Place the twisted length on your pan, around the edge of the circle. Join by cutting the two ends diagonally, moistening with water, and pressing together.

BRAIDED WREATH

This is formed in the same way as the twisted wreath, but with three rolls of dough braided together. Roll out three long snakes of dough, their length three times the diameter of your pan, and braid them, taking care to keep the shape of the braid even. A good way to prevent the braid from becoming thick at one end and thin at the other is to start braiding at the center and work out toward the ends. Place on a round baking sheet and join as for the twisted wreath.

$\mathscr{D}$ough baskets can be fashioned in many different ways, and can be either wall-hanging or free-standing. The projects in this book use basic flat wall-hanging baskets in different shapes and with different types of weave patterns.

BASKET-WEAVE EFFECT
Use a wooden skewer to press lines into the dough.

FINEWEAVE EFFECT
Use a fork to make evenly spaced lines across the basket, then drawing a wooden skewer down over them to form the vertical lines.

WOVEN STRIPS
Roll your dough out to ¼ inch (6mm) thick, and, using the straight edge of a ruler to guide your knife, cut strips of dough approximately ½ inch (12 mm) wide. Then, attach the vertical strips to your basket base using a little water, and carefully weave the horizontal strips through. Trim off the edges neatly with a knife when you have finished. A small twist of dough at the bottom adds the finishing touch.

SEASHELL DESIGN
Use small seafood forks to make vertical lines down the basket.

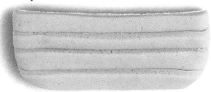

A SOLID BASE
An overlapping style of basket can be created by building up a layer of overlapping strips on top of a rolled-out base. It is particularly suitable for larger projects that require a more substantial basket.

BASKET HANDLES
Basket handles are produced by rolling long snakes of dough, twisting them together, then attaching to the basic basket shape using a little water on the seams. To finish, attach a small twist at the base of your basket to act as a pedestal.

To make any of the baskets in this book, roll out a sheet of dough ⅜ inch (10mm) thick and cut to shape from one of the many templates found in the back of the book (see pages 120–22).

2
ANIMALS

MICE AND PORCUPINES

These cute animals are the simplest of all the projects and can be made in a few minutes. The ideal size is about 2–3 inches (51–76mm) long, but it is fun to make families of them in a variety of sizes. Although the little creatures in the photographs are left in the natural dough finish, you can also paint them for more interesting variety.

To make the mice and porcupines shown, you will need:

- *2 cups flour made into dough (see page 11)*
- *Wooden skewer or toothpick*
- *Black-headed pushpins or cloves*
- *Small pointed scissors*
- *Varnish*

MOUSE

1 Take a ball of dough of the size you want your mouse to be and roll it smoothly. Roll one end between the palms of your hands to give the conical shape of the mouse's pointed nose. Lay dough on a baking sheet.

2 Make two ears from small balls of dough flattened between the fingers and pinched together at the base. Dampen and attach them to the mouse's body, toward the nose. Mark eyes with a skewer or toothpick. Roll a long piece of "spaghetti" dough, tuck one end under the mouse's bottom, and bring the rest of the tail up over its body, curling it around – the dough is not strong enough to leave the tail sticking out.

3 Bake and varnish as instructed in Basic Techniques.

PORCUPINE

1 Follow step 1 as for the mouse.

2 Holding the body in the palm of one hand, use small, sharp scissors to snip spines all over the body beginning about ⅜ inch (10mm) from the nose. Work diagonally across the body to avoid cutting the spines in rows – this would be obvious on the finished piece. Mark the eyes with a toothpick or skewer, and push a black-headed pushpin into the end of the nose. If you haven't one of these, a black glass-headed dressmaker's pin or small clove will serve just as well.

3 Bake and varnish as instructed in Basic Techniques.

These rather comical ginger tomcats are quite simply made, and, as with the mice and porcupines, are fun in families. Why not try a mother cat with an assortment of different-colored kittens?

To make two cats, you will need:

- *2 cups flour made into dough (see page 11)*
- *Wooden skewer or toothpick*
- *Black-headed pushpins*
- *Paper clips*
- *Paint*
- *Varnish*

LYING CAT

1 Roll a smooth golfball-sized ball of dough and flatten it slightly for the body. Add two small pea-sized balls of dough for the paws.

2 Add a smaller, slightly flattened ball of dough for the head, and pinch two small pieces of dough between thumb and index finger to form the ears. Dampen the base of the ears and attach them to the top of the head. For the facial detail, add two small flattened balls of dough for the cheeks and a black-headed pushpin for the nose. Mark the whiskers and eyes using a toothpick or skewer.

3 Add a long sausage of dough, pointed at one end, and slip it under the body at the back, curling it around to form the tail. Mark claws in the paws with a toothpick.

4 Bake, paint as desired, and varnish as instructed in Basic Techniques.

SITTING CAT

1 Form the body and head as for the lying cat. Attach together and add facial details as shown below.

2 Add rolls of dough for legs, with a small ball of dough at the base of each leg for the paws. Mark the claws as before.

3 Add a tail as shown.

4 Push a small paper clip into the ball of the head to form a hanger. Bake, paint as desired, and varnish as instructed in Basic Techniques. Cats can be painted in any color – a striped cat is very effective, as shown in the photograph.

*D*ucks are an ever-popular subject, and these would be equally suitable for a kitchen, bathroom, or child's bedroom. They can be made and displayed individually or as a group. Why not try three ducks flying across the wall?

The mother duck and ducklings are made in the same way, but in different sizes.

To make the complete group, you will need:

- *2 cups flour made into dough (see page 11)*
- *Wooden skewer or toothpick*
- *Cloves*
- *Scissors*
- *Paper clips*
- *Paint*
- *Varnish*

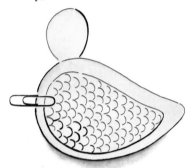

Paint ribbon strings for duckling

1 To make each duckling, take a piece of dough the size of a golf ball, and roll it into a smooth cone shape. Press flat and lay on baking sheet. Repeat with a slightly smaller piece of dough for the wing, marking the feathers with the end of a paper clip. Lay this on top of the body.

2 With a little water, attach an egg-shaped piece of dough approximately the size of a grape for the head. Form a small cone of dough for the beak and snip the pointed end open with the scissors. Moisten and attach to the front of the head.

4 Add the bow by placing two small triangles of dough, pointed ends together, at the duckling's neck, as shown. The ribbons hanging from the bow are painted on the chest after baking. Mark the eye with a skewer. Last, push a small paper clip well into the dough just behind the head for the hanging ribbon.

5 To make the mother duck, use an orange-sized ball of dough for the body, and increase the size of the other pieces proportionally. Use a clove for the eye and add two feet instead of one.

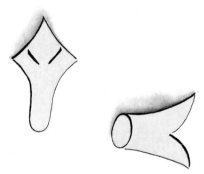

Dough ribbon strings for mother duck

3 For the feet, make a small, thin cone of dough, flatten it, and shape the end to a point with your fingers. Moisten the top end of the foot and, lifting the body gently, slip it underneath. Mark the foot webs with a toothpick or skewer.

6 Cut two long, thin triangles of flattened dough for the ribbons at mother duck's neck and attach them to the body, thin ends touching the bow as shown.

7 Bake, paint beaks and feet yellow, and bows and ribbons in the color of your choice. Varnish as instructed in Basic Techniques.

PIGS AND PIGLETS

*T*hese delightful pigs are made by combining the skills of rolling and cutting dough with hand modeling. The pigs can be plain, painted to give a spotted effect, or even painted pink for fun. A thick black marking pen makes easy work of adding spots. If you want a darker finish, for a brown pig or a saddleback, for example, turn the oven up to 300°F (150°C) for about 1 hour after baking is complete, or add some brown spice, powder paint, or food coloring to the raw dough.

To make all these pigs, you will need:
- *2 cups flour made into dough (see page 11)*
- *Wooden skewer or toothpick*
- *Sharp knife*
- *Paper clips*
- *Paint*
- *Varnish*

LARGE AND SMALL PIGS

1 Roll out half your dough to approximately ¼ inch (6mm) thickness and using the templates (see page 118), cut out the basic shape. To form the body of the pig, roll a slightly oval ball of dough and flatten it. Dampen the base and lay the body on the top half, completely covering the upper edge. Roll a smaller ball of dough and flatten for the head, dampen it, and attach it to body.

2 For the features, add a small ball of dough for the nose and press a slight hollow in it, using the blunt end of a pencil or the handle of a wooden spoon. Mark the eyes and nostrils with a skewer or toothpick. For the ears, roll two small sausages of dough, flatten them, and attach with a little water to the top of the head as shown, bending them over to lie on the face.

3 Add a small curly tail and mark the feet with a knife. The larger pig looks more realistic if you cut away some of the dough to form the legs. Push a paper clip into the top for hanging, and position it slightly toward the head of the pig so that he doesn't do a nosedive when you hang him on the wall.

4 Bake, paint as desired, and varnish as instructed in Basic Techniques.

MOTHER PIG AND PIGLETS

1 These are made as the single pig, but instead of legs we add piglets. Use the template (see page 118). Note that the template for the base of the mother pig is much shorter than that for the standing pig because she is lying down.

2 Proceed as for the single pig as far as step 3 and add a small curly tail. Then add two sausage-shaped front legs and mark the feet with a knife.

3 Add the piglets by dampening the base and laying four small balls of dough against the mother's belly. The creases are made with a wooden skewer or toothpick, and a small piece of spaghetti dough is attached to each to make a curly little tail.

4 Push a paper clip into the top for hanging. Bake, paint as desired, and varnish as instructed in Basic Techniques.

SHEEP FAMILY

This family of ewe, ram, and wooly lambs is great fun to make. Although the process is simple, the results are very effective.

To make the complete sheep family, you will need:

- *3 cups flour made into dough (see page 11)*
- *Knife*
- *Potato ricer (preferably) or garlic press*
- *Wooden skewer or toothpick*
- *Cloves*
- *Paper clips*
- *Paint*
- *Varnish*

1 Roll an oval ball of dough and flatten it for the body. Take a smaller piece for the head and make it slightly pointed at the mouth. Dampen and attach to the body.

2 To make the legs, roll out a long, thin sausage of dough, cut off the required length, fold in half and attach to the body as shown. Mark the feet with a knife. If you are making a ram, add horns made from rolled-up dough.

3 This is the fun part. Using a potato ricer (this is a very labor-intensive process with a garlic press), make a heap of extruded dough and cut into approximately ¾-inch (19mm) lengths. Brush the body with water and attach the "wool" all over, including the top of the head.

4 Add pointed ears, sticking out sideways not upward, in front of the horns if you have them. Finally, mark the eyes and nostrils with a wooden skewer or toothpick. Cloves can be used for eyes on the bigger sheep.

5 Add a paper clip for hanging, estimating the center of gravity to make sure your sheep hangs correctly. (Often the clip is a little closer to the head.) Bake, paint as desired, and varnish as instructed in Basic Techniques.

TEDDY BEAR AND RABBIT

These two delightful figures make lovely decorations for a children's room. The teddy is designed along the lines of a traditional jointed bear, and the rabbit was inspired by Beatrix Potter's Flopsy Bunnies.

For each of these animals, you will need:

- *1 cup flour made into dough (see page 11)*
- *Wooden skewer or toothpick*
- *Black-headed pushpins or cloves*
- *Sharp knife*
- *Paper clip*
- *Paint*
- *Varnish*

TEDDY BEAR

1 Roll a smooth oval ball of dough for the body, dampen, and add a smaller round ball for the head. Then, add an even smaller one for the muzzle.

2 Add sausages of dough for the arms and legs, shaping the legs a little as you roll them. The pads are marked with a skewer or toothpick. (The ones on the feet can be marked by pressing the end of a cake decorating tip into the dough, if you have one of suitable size.)

3 Add ears made from small balls of dough flattened between thumb and index finger and pinched together at the base. The eyes and nose are pushpins or cloves. Mark the mouth and a navel with a skewer, and add a dough bow with ribbons at the neck.

4 Push a paper clip into the top of the head for hanging. Bake, paint as desired, and varnish according to instructions in Basic Techniques.

RABBIT

1 The head and body of the rabbit are made from two flattened pear-shaped pieces of dough, joined together with water.

2 Two sausage-shaped hind legs are added, one slipped under the body, the other laid on top. A smaller sausage is added for the arm and a ball of dough, roughened with a sharp knife, for the tail.

3 For the facial detail, add two long, pointed ears, moistened and firmly attached to the top of the head. Use a pushpin for the nose, a clove for the eye, and mark whiskers with the point of a sharp knife.

4 Finally, add a bow at the neck as for the teddy, and a paper clip for hanging. Bake, paint, and varnish as instructed in Basic Techniques.

*M*any people are collectors of frogs or owls, and one of these little comic characters would make a lovely gift. Frogs are quite a difficult subject to model, but this very simple, stylized version, designed by my friend Linda Allen, is really quite easy to make. To add interest, you can sit him on a dough lily pad – a group of them together can look quite hilarious. You almost expect them to start hopping across the room.

To make a collection of animals, you will need:

- *1 cup flour made into dough (see page 11)*
- *Black-headed pushpins*
- *Sharp knife*
- *Small pointed scissors*
- *Paper clips*
- *Paint*
- *Varnish*

FROG

1 Make an oval-shaped body and add a small ball of dough for the head. Try to blend the dough together so that the seam doesn't show too much.

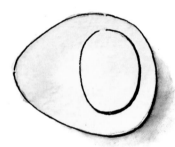

2 To add facial detail, use thumb and index finger to pinch up the dough to form the eye recesses. Push in two pushpins for eyes. Mark the nostrils and a nice wide smiling mouth with a skewer or toothpick.

3 Lift the body slightly and slip under two little front feet made from flattened dough sausages. For the hind legs, add two long, thin rolls, meeting at the back of the body and brought around to the front, ending in flattened feet. Cut the toes with a knife.

4 Bake, paint as desired, and varnish according to the instructions in Basic Techniques.

OWL

1 Make an inverted pear-shaped ball of dough and flatten it slightly for the owl body. Pinch the top corners between thumb and index finger to form the ears. You may need to play around a little to achieve just the right shape. Add two small, thin, flattened inverted teardrop shapes for the wings, and either mark the feathers with the loop of a paper clip or snip with scissors. Dot in the breast feathers with a skewer or toothpick, and mark the tail feathers with a knife.

2 Add two eyes made from balls of dough that have been flattened and cut into a circle. Push a hole in the center of each eye and mark spoke lines around with a knife. Place a small triangular beak between the eyes.

3 Add two small, flattened triangular feet, and mark the claws with a toothpick.

4 Add a paper clip at the head for hanging. Bake, paint as desired, and varnish according to the instructions in Basic Techniques.

COW AND PONY

*P*onies are big favorites with children, and this one was designed at the request of my horse-loving daughters. The cow is of the same basic construction, and both animals can be painted in a variety of different colors to depict different breeds.

To make a cow and pony, you will need:

- *2 cups flour made into dough (see page 11)*
- *Cloves*
- *Garlic press or potato ricer*
- *Wooden skewer or toothpick*
- *Paper clips*
- *Paint*
- *Varnish*

COW

1 Roll out a fat sausage of dough and flatten it to form the body. Pinch one of the top corners into a point to form the prominent hip bone. Using the first two fingers of your right hand (if you are right-handed) and working against the palm of your left hand, roll out a thin piece of dough for each of the legs. The curved area where your two fingers meet will form a ridge in the dough making a perfect knee joint. Slip the first two legs underneath the body.

wooden skewer. Using a knife, make hair marks in the top knot and end of the tail.

5 Push a paper-clip hanger into the back of the cow, trying to make sure it will hang straight once baked. It takes a certain amount of guesswork initially to find the right spot, but with a little practice you will soon get it right. Bake, paint, and varnish as instructed in Basic Techniques.

2 Add a small ball of dough for the udder and then two more legs, this time attached to the top of the body with a little water. Roll a long, thin piece of dough with a wider piece at one end for the tail and attach to the cow's rear, making sure that the tail touches the body and legs all the way down since it will break if it is left sticking out.

3 Make an inverted pear shape for the head. Moisten it and attach to the body. Add pointed ears sticking out at right angles to the head.

4 Finally, add a pinched piece of dough for the top knot, cloves for eyes, and mark nostrils with a

PONY

1 Form the body in the same way as the cow but without the prominent pelvic bone. Pinch or stretch dough to make an elongated neck.

2 Add the legs as for the cow, omitting the udder. Place an inverted pear-shaped head at the top of the neck.

3 Using dough extruded through a potato ricer or garlic press, add a long tail and a mane all the way down the neck. A small fringe of extruded dough forms the forelock.

4 Make the ears, which are smaller than the cow's and point up, and attach with a little water. Nostrils are made with a wooden skewer, and cloves are added for eyes.

5 Push a paper-clip hanger into the back of the pony as you did for the cow, then bake, paint, and varnish as instructed in Basic Techniques.

3
WREATHS

FRUIT TWIST AND GRAPE RING

*T*hese wreaths are quick and easy to produce. The grapes can be painted almost any color without looking strange, which is useful if you want to match a particular color scheme.

To make two small wreaths, you will need:

- *2 cups flour made into dough (see page 11)*
- *Knife*
- *Cloves*
- *Baking pan, 6 to 8-inch (152 to 203 mm) diameter*
- *Paper clips*
- *Paint*
- *Varnish*

FRUIT TWIST

1 Following the instructions in Basic Techniques (page 22), make a small twisted wreath, working about ¾ inch (19mm) inside the outer edge of your baking pan. Place three cut leaves over the seam in the wreath and then add an apple and pear.

2 Fill in the spaces around the apple and pear with plums and berries.

3 Add a sturdy paper-clip hanger directly opposite the fruit, taking care to bury it well in the dough but without pushing it right through. Bake, paint as desired, and varnish.

GRAPE RING

1 Form the twisted wreath in the same way as for the Fruit Twist, but this time position the seam at the top of the wreath. Add three molded leaves to cover this point.

2 Make a large bundle of small balls of dough for the grapes (see page 16) and, after moistening the garland, lift them into place to cascade down the side. Add a couple of pieces of spaghetti dough twisted to look like vines.

3 Add a paper-clip hanger and then bake, paint as desired, and varnish.

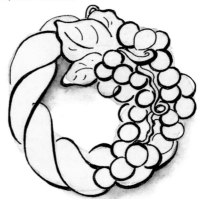

Fruit and Vegetable Wreaths

These traditional wreaths make perfect kitchen decorations. They can be made in varying sizes to suit your requirements. Simply add more or less fruit to the basic wreath as shown in the photographs.

For a larger-size wreath, you will need:

- *2 cups flour made into dough (see page 11)*
- *Wooden skewer or toothpick*
- *Cloves*
- *Baking pan, 9-inch (230cm) diameter*
- *Large paper clip*
- *Paint*
- *Varnish*

FRUIT WREATH

1 Following the instructions in Basic Techniques (page 22), lay a long sausage of dough around a circular baking pan and flatten slightly. Roll 12 balls of dough and flatten into leaves. Mark veins with a skewer and place on top of the dough circle.

2 Add two pears, two apples, and two oranges as shown in the diagram. Then place two molded leaves, five strawberries, and a strawberry flower to the left of the main bunch of fruit, and a molded leaf and a bunch of grapes to the right. Fill in any spaces between the fruit with plums and berries.

3 Push a very large paper-clip hanger into the top of the garland. Bake, paint as desired, and varnish as instructed in Basic Techniques.

For the smaller garlands, use a 7-inch (178mm) baking pan and make a garland with nine leaves. Add less fruit and vegetables, as shown in the photographs.

VEGETABLE WREATH

1 Proceed as in step 1 for the Fruit Wreath.

2 Add the cauliflower, cabbage, and potatoes (made as instructed in Basic Techniques) at the bottom of the wreath, as shown in the diagram. The reason for this is that while the fruit needs to be at the top so that the bunch of grapes can hang down, the leeks and carrots look better growing up.

3 Place a bunch of leeks on one side of these vegetables and a bunch of carrots on the other. Finally, fill in any spaces with mushrooms and tomatoes. When you arrange your vegetables, bear in mind their colors when they are finished, and don't put items of the same or similar colors, such as leeks and cauliflower or tomatoes and carrots, next to each other.

4 Push a very large paper-clip hanger into the top of your wreath. Bake, paint, and varnish.

Small Fruit Wreath, top; Vegetable Wreath, middle; Large Fruit Wreath, bottom.

ROSE WREATH

This variation is a decorative design for a bedroom or living room. The roses can be painted to match your decor and can be added singly or in clusters, depending on the size of wreath you want.

The large and small wreaths made in the same way, with extra roses for the larger version.

For one large rose wreath, you will need:

- *2 cups flour made into dough (see page 11)*
- *Wooden skewer or toothpick*
- *Baking pan, 9-inch (230mm) diameter*
- *Paper clip*
- *Paint*
- *Varnish*

1 On your baking sheet, form a wreath using 12 balls of dough flattened into leaves approximately 2 inches (50mm) in diameter, following the instructions in Basic Techniques (page 22).

2 Refer to page 17 and form nine slightly smaller leaves with pointed ends and arrange on the wreath as shown.

3 Form nine full-blown roses, each approximately 1 inch (25mm) across, using the method explained in Basic Techniques (page 17). Lay them in clusters, placing each rose between the rose leaves as shown. Add nine buds, made by rolling one or two petals tightly, placing one between each rose.

4 Push a large paper clip into the top of your wreath, directly opposite the center group of roses. Bake, paint in colors of your choice, and varnish as instructed in Basic Techniques.

For the smaller-size wreath (top left and right), use a 7-inch (178mm) baking pan and place nine leaves around the garland. Add one full-blown rose and three buds to each group of rose leaves.

This wreath is more intricate than those with the leaves, and the result is more delicate. Take care when painting this project, and use a small brush for the tiny berries and flowers.

To make this wreath, you will need:

- *2 cups flour made into dough (see page 11)*
- *Wooden skewer or toothpick*
- *Cloves*
- *Baking pan, 9-inch (230mm) diameter*
- *Large paper clip*
- *Paint*
- *Varnish*

1 Make a braided wreath as instructed in Basic Techniques (page 22), and place six leaves over the seam at the bottom.

2 Add an apple, orange, and pear in the center of this group of leaves, then place a cluster of strawberries on one side and plums on the other.

3 Fill in the spaces between the fruits with berries, and then place small leaves, small flowers, and berries, either individually or in twos and threes, all around the wreath, tucking them in between the ropes of the braid.

4 Push a large paper clip for hanging into the wreath opposite the main bunch of fruit, making sure that it does not pierce through the dough. Bake, paint as desired, and varnish as instructed in Basic Techniques.

*S*alt dough lends itself wonderfully to bread sculpture. Adding a few stalks of wheat and a leaf or two lightens this wreath and makes a superb kitchen decoration.

To make this wreath you will need:

- *3 cups flour made into dough (see page 11)*
- *Cloves*
- *Small scissors*
- *Wooden skewer or toothpick*
- *Baking pan, 9-inch (230mm) diameter*
- *Sesame seeds and poppy seeds*
- *Giant paper clip*
- *Paint*
- *Varnish*

1 Make a wreath as for the Braided Wreath (page 50) with fruit and flowers project. Working with the seam at the top and following the instructions in Basic Techniques, make three French loaves and lay them over the seam. Add two cottage loaves, two peasant loaves, and two knots, around the ring (see Basic Techniques).

2 Add groups of three sesame seed buns between each loaf, alternating between the inside edge and outside edge of the ring. Add pairs of wheat stalks opposite the sesame buns, again alternating between the inside and outside edges of the wreath.

3 Finally, add a few small leaves dotted between the loaves, and fill in any spaces with a small ball of dough with a clove pushed into the center.

4 Push a giant paper clip well into the dough, as this is a particularly heavy piece and needs a strong hanger. Bake, paint the leaves if desired, and varnish as instructed in Basic Techniques.

These heart-shaped versions of the basic fruit and rose wreaths make a superb gift for a wedding or anniversary, as well as Valentine's Day. To personalize the gift, you could add a banner of dough across the wreath with a date or initials.

To make either heart, you will need:

- *2 cups flour made into dough (see page 11)*
- *Wooden skewer or toothpick*
- *Cloves*
- *Giant paper clip*
- *Paint*
- *Varnish*

1 Use the traced template on page 119 as a guide. If you prefer, trace the template on baking parchment, place it on your baking sheet and work directly on it. Roll out two sausages of dough each approximately ¾ inch (19mm) in diameter and 10 inches (254mm) long. Place these around the edges of the template to form the two sides of the heart. Flatten them slightly and then place 14 molded leaves along the wreath.

2 For the fruit wreath, add two apples, two pears, and two oranges in the center of the heart as shown. Place a leaf and five strawberries with a flower on the left, and a leaf with a bunch of grapes on the right. Fill in any spaces with plums and berries.

3 For the rose heart, place a cluster of full-blown roses in the center of the heart and add some pointed leaves around the edges and in between some of the roses. Fill in any spaces with rosebuds made as instructed in Basic Techniques (page 17). Add a giant paper clip for a hanger in the center of the wreath.

4 If you wish to add a banner, roll out a strip of dough ¼ inch (6mm) thick and cut a 1-inch (25mm) wide ribbon. The center of the banner will need to be supported to prevent it from drooping in the middle. Crumple a piece of foil to form a bridge across the heart. To write on the banner, use the pointed end of a skewer or a toothpick, and prick the letters into the dough rather than dragging the stick across it.

5 Bake, paint as desired, and varnish as instructed in Basic Techniques.

All sorts of nuts, seed pods, and pine-cones gathered in the fall make lovely decorations for a piece of dough. They are simply brushed with water and pressed into the raw dough. Once baked, they are firmly anchored in place, ready for varnishing. More delicate items, such as dried flowers or stalks of wheat, may be attached after varnishing with all-purpose glue.

To make an autumn wreath, you will need:

- *2 cups flour made into dough (see page 11)*
- *Baking pan, 9-inch (230mm) diameter*
- *Selection of nuts, cones, seeds, grasses, dried or silk*
- *flowers, etc.*
- *Large paper clip*
- *Varnish*

1 The base of the wreath can be any type of ring you like. Generally speaking, a thicker wreath, such as a braided ring or one with leaves, is preferable, as it provides better support for your decoration.

2 Make the wreath of your choice following the instructions in Basic Techniques (page 22), and then simply add your decoration, leaving as much or as little of the dough showing as you desire.

3 A simpler flat cut-out ring can look attractive with a few stalks of wheat glued to it, and perhaps a little mouse crawling up the side.

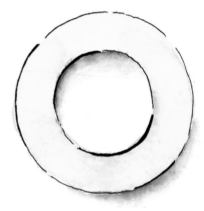

4 Push a large paper clip into the top for a hanger. Bake and varnish as instructed in Basic Techniques. Glue any dried or delicate material in place after the varnish has dried.

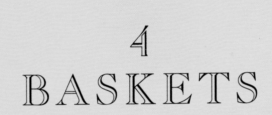

4
BASKETS

FRUIT BASKETS

Choose any fruit to make these simple baskets and coordinate them with your decor. The baskets are shown in a choice of sizes, and the templates for cutting them can be found on pages 120–22.

To make one large and one small basket, you will need:

- *2 cups flour made into dough (see page 11)*
- *Wooden skewer or toothpick*
- *Cloves*
- *Large paper clips*
- *Paint*
- *Varnish*

1 Following the instructions given in Basic Techniques and using a template on pages 120–22, make a basket. Using a wooden skewer or toothpick, mark the basket weave. For the large basket, make 12 leaves and, using a little water, attach them to the basket as shown in the diagram.

3 Push a large paper clip between the two central top leaves for hanging – this takes the pressure off the handle when you hang your dough on the wall. This is not necessary with the small basket, as it is much lighter and the handle is thin enough to hang on a picture nail. Bake, paint as desired, and varnish as instructed in Basic Techniques.

2 Make the fruit of your choice as instructed in Basic Techniques, and place it on the basket in the center of the leaves (see photo facing page). Add a few extra cut leaves tucked in between the pieces of fruit.

The small basket is made in exactly the same way, but with everything scaled down and with seven leaves instead of 12 around the edge of the fruit.

MIXED FRUIT BASKET

This luxurious and colorful basket of fruit is based on the Fruit Basket project and is made using exactly the same method.

To make the mixed fruit basket, you will need:

- 2 cups flour made into dough (see page 11)
- Wooden skewer or toothpick
- Cloves
- Large paper clip
- Paint
- Varnish

1 Using the template on page 121, make your basket as instructed in Basic Techniques (page 23). Make about 20 leaves, moisten with a little water, and position them around the basket.

2 Make two each of the following fruits – apples, oranges, pears, and lemons. Arrange them on the basket as shown in the diagram.

3 Add a cluster of strawberries and a strawberry flower on one side of the basket, and a bunch of grapes spilling out of the basket on the other side. Fill in the spaces between the fruits with berries, plums, and a few small leaves.

4 Push a large paper clip into the center of the fruit at the top to take the pressure off the handle when it hangs on the wall. Bake, paint, and varnish as instructed in Basic Techniques.

SUMMER FRUIT BASKETS

These lovely summery projects are very similar to the simple fruit baskets, but the extra detail makes them a little more interesting, and the bright color makes a particularly eye-catching piece.

To make one of these baskets, you will need:

- *2 cups flour made into dough (see page 11)*
- *Fork*
- *Cloves (for the strawberries)*
- *Florist's wire (for the cherries)*
- *Large paper clip*
- *Paint*
- *Varnish*

1 Using the template on page 120, make a basket as instructed in Basic Techniques (page 23). Mark the weave using the prongs of a fork. Make 12 leaves and position them around the basket as shown in the diagram.

3 Add a few small leaves and small flowers dotted among the fruit.

2 Make and add your fruit, heaping it onto the basket for a luxurious effect. For the strawberry basket, make some of the strawberries with the star-shaped stalk on top and the rest with a headless clove pushed into them as shown in Basic Techniques (page 16). For the cherry basket, make holes in the cherries with a toothpick and add pieces of florist's wire cut approximately 2 inches (50mm) long. Bend a few of them into a slight curve to form a stalk.

4 Push a large paper clip into the center of the fruit at the top for hanging. Bake, paint, and varnish as instructed in Basic Techniques.

ROSE BASKET

This project is a more advanced version of the Strawberry and Cherry Baskets. If you find the basket weaving too complicated, you could use one of the simpler styles, such as that used for the fruit baskets. The roses can be painted in a variety of colors or in several different shades of the same color.

To make the rose basket, you will need:

- *2 cups flour made into dough (see page 11)*
- *Sharp knife*
- *Wooden skewer or toothpick*
- *Large paper clip*
- *Paint*
- *Varnish*

1 Using the template on page 122, make a woven basket as instructed in Basic Techniques, covering the bottom half of the template base below the dotted line with the woven strips. Using a little water to attach them, place molded rose leaves all around the top edge of the base and across the top of the basket as shown in the diagram.

2 Fill in the top of the base with full-blown roses, made according to the instructions in Basic Techniques (page 17). Be careful not to pack them so tight that they get squashed.

3 Add several small leaves between the roses, and fill in any remaining spaces with buds.

4 Push a large paper clip for hanging into the center of the model at the top, making sure it is secure. Bake, paint, and varnish as instructed in Basic Techniques.

BREAD BASKET

*A*lthough it contains little color, this piece is extremely attractive and makes a stunning kitchen decoration. The basket also matches the Bread and Wheat Ring in Chapter 3 and, together, they make an attractive pair.

To make the bread basket, you will need:

- *2 cups flour made into dough (see page 11)*
- *Poppy and sesame seeds*
- *Fork and small scissors*
- *Wooden skewer or toothpick*
- *Cloves*
- *Paper clip*
- *Paint and varnish*

1 Roll out half the dough to ¼ inch (6mm) thickness and follow the template on page 121 to make a basket, using the prongs of a fork to create the weave as shown in Basic Techniques (page 23).

Clockwise from top left, above: two knots, two peasant loaves, three French loaves, two cottage loaves, three sesame seed buns, three poppy seed rolls.

2 Assemble the bows by placing two thick triangles of dough at each end of the handle and adding the ribbons cut from a flattened piece of dough as shown in the diagram.

3 Make the bread to fill the basket according to the instructions in Basic Techniques (pages 20–21).

4 Assemble the bread in the basket as shown in the photograph. Fill in the spaces between the loaves with stalks of wheat, small leaves, and small balls of dough with a clove pressed into the center.

5 Add a large paper clip in the center of the basket for hanging. Bake, then paint the bows in the color of your choice, the leaves green, and then varnish as instructed in Basic Techniques.

BASKET COLLAGE

As with the Autumn Wreath, this is a simple project using salt dough as a basis for a collection of real nuts, spices, seed pods and pinecones.

To make the basket collage, you will need:

- *1 cup flour made into dough (see page 11)*
- *Wooden skewer or toothpick*
- *Knife*
- *Selection of nuts, cones, grasses, dried flowers, etc.*
- *Large paper clip*
- *Varnish*

1 Using the template on page 120, make a simple basket with leaves added to it, as instructed in the Fruit Baskets project (see page 60).

3 Push a paper-clip hanger into the top of your basket. Bake, then varnish as instructed in Basic Techniques.

2 Arrange your collection of nuts, seed pods, cones, etc., on the basket, making sure that you have moistened them with water. Once baked, they will be firmly attached to the dough. Spices, such as pieces of cinnamon stick and star anise, add variety and interest. Fill in any spaces with small leaves, and/or small balls of dough with a clove pushed into the center.

An alternative to the method used above involves using all-purpose adhesive to glue dried flowers or grasses to a plain baked basket.

VEGETABLE BASKET

These vegetables look almost good enough to eat. This project needs particular care in judging the center of gravity so the basket doesn't hang awkwardly on the wall.

To make the vegetable basket, you will need:

- *2 cups flour made into dough (see page 11)*
- *Small cloves*
- *Garlic press*
- *Wooden skewer or toothpick*
- *Giant paper clip*
- *Paint*
- *Varnish*

1 Using the template on page 119, make the flat basket with overlapped strips of dough as instructed in Basic Techniques (page 23). Mark the center of the basket and immediately to the left of the center, place a rolled piece of dough 3 × 1 inch (76 × 25mm), as shown in the diagram. This forms a base for the handle.

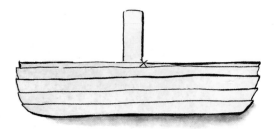

2 Roll a strip of dough 1 inch (25mm) wide by approximately 9 inches (230mm) long. Lay it on the baking sheet adjacent to the handle base. Fold over and lay the remainder of the strip on top of the handle base, continuing across the center of the basket, as shown in the diagram. Trim the end even with the base of the basket.

3 Make a selection of vegetables, (as shown in the photograph) according to the instructions in Basic Techniques (page 18), and lay them along the top edge of the basket, making sure that they are dampened slightly and are touching the top of the

basket. Begin at the center, with the cabbage resting on the handle, then add the potatoes and leeks. Place the tomatoes between and slightly on top of the potatoes and leeks.

4 Next, beginning with the carrots, work out from the center on the left-hand side of the basket, adding the cauliflower and green beans. Place a few mushrooms between and slightly overlapping the cauliflower and beans. You may, of course, substitute other vegetables of your choice.

5 Push a giant paper clip into the top of the handle for hanging, making sure it is well embedded in the dough. Bake, paint, and varnish as instructed in Basic Techniques.

CORNUCOPIA

This glorious horn of plenty with fruit spilling over the edge is assembled from relatively simple individual pieces. The overlapped style of basket produces a heavier base to counterbalance the mass of fruit at the top.

1 Roll out half the dough to approximately ¼-inch (6mm) thickness and then, using the template on page 122, cut out the basic horn shape and place it on your baking sheet.

To make the cornucopia you will need:
- *3 cups flour made into dough (see page 11)*
- *Cloves*
- *Knife*
- *Wooden skewer or toothpick*
- *Giant paper clip*
- *Paint*
- *Varnish*

2 Reroll the trimmings and cut into strips approximately ½ inch (13mm) wide at one end and ¾ inch (19mm) wide at the other end. The longest strip needed is 8 inches (203mm). Using the template as a guide and starting at the dotted line, lay the strips overlapping each other down to the point of the horn, with the narrower ends along the curved inside edge of the horn. Once the bottom half of the base is covered, trim the strips level with the base.

5 Place the apple, oranges, and pears in position (see Basic Techniques), then the five strawberries. Dot the seeds on the strawberries with a skewer after positioning them. Add one or two small flowers to the group of strawberries.

6 Place grapes in the space between the pineapple and the other fruit. Making a pile of grapes and placing them in position as a group rather than individually will achieve a more natural effect.

3 Lay leaves around the edge as shown.

4 Form the pineapple by flattening an oval ball of dough and marking diagonal lines in both directions with the back of a knife. Push a clove, without the seed head into each square. The leaves are formed by flattening thin pointed strips.

7 Last, lay the stalks of wheat alongside the fruit and fill in any spaces with plums or berries, bearing in mind the colors you will be painting them. Add a couple of twists of vine to the grapes and along the basket.

8 Push a giant paper clip for hanging into the top of the pineapple. Bake, paint, and varnish as instructed in Basic Techniques.

5
PLANTS
AND TREES

MUSHROOMS

This simple project can be made by a beginner. The mushrooms may be left natural or painted, and as many as you like may be grouped in clusters for a variety of shapes and sizes. Children can easily make a single mushroom or toadstool and might like to paint it in bright colors.

To make the basic group of five mushrooms, you will need:

- *1 cup flour made into dough (see page 11)*
- *Garlic press or potato ricer*
- *Knife*
- *Paper clip*
- *Paint*
- *Varnish*

1 Roll out a long sausage of dough and cut into five stem pieces – one 2½ inches (64mm) long, two 3 inches (76mm) long, one 4 inches (102mm) long and one 5 inches (127mm) long. Arrange them together on your baking sheet as shown, laying the shortest piece centrally on top of the others.

2 Form the tops of the second and central toadstools by taking a golf-ball-sized piece of dough, rolling it into a smooth ball, and gently working a hollow center with your thumb. Place one of these on the top ends of the stalks.

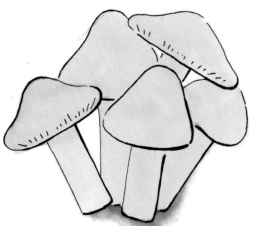

3 Form the flat mushroom tops by taking a slightly smaller ball of dough and working it into a flat head, slightly pointed on the top. Moisten the ends of the first and third stalks and attach the heads. Mark the gills on the underside of these flat mushrooms using a sharp knife. Finally, to produce a button mushroom for the last stalk, take a ball of dough 1 inch (25mm) in diameter and press a hollow center with your thumb.

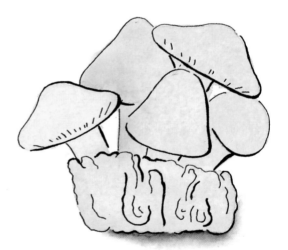

4 Add extruded dough pressed through a garlic press or potato ricer at the base for grass, and a paper clip at the top for hanging. Bake, paint if desired, and varnish as instructed in Basic Techniques.

TREES

The number of different designs for trees is almost endless. Simply follow the instructions in Basic Techniques (page 19) and create your own combination of trunk, leaves, and pot. The designs illustrated are an apple and bay tree.

To make one tree, you will need:

- *2 cups flour made into dough (see page 11)*
- *Potato ricer or garlic press*
- *Paper clip*
- *Paint*
- *Varnish*

APPLE TREE

1 Make a split trunk approximately 8 inches (203mm) long, as shown in Basic Techniques. Separate the branches at the top and place a number of flattened balls of dough around the branches.

2 Cover each ball of dough with pinched leaves and dot the leaves with small pea-sized apples.

3 Finish the base of the tree with a mound of extruded dough grass.

4 Push a paper-clip hanger into the top of the tree. Bake, paint, and varnish as instructed in Basic Techniques.

BAY TREE

1 The trunk here is simply a roll of dough 6 inches (152mm) long which can be twisted slightly to make it look more natural. Place a flattened ball of dough approximately 3 inches (76mm) in diameter at the top of the trunk and cut a dough flowerpot for the bottom. Make sure that the trunk extends below the pot and into the top of the tree.

2 Make many small, molded leaves approximately 1 inch (25mm) long, and place them all the way around the edge of the tree top as shown. Fill the rest of the tree top with leaves arranged like the petals of a flower.

3 Push a paper-clip hanger into the top of the tree to hang it on the wall. Bake, paint, and varnish as instructed in Basic Techniques.

PARTRIDGE IN A PEAR TREE

*T*his is really just a tree with a bird in it, but it does remind me of the Christmas carol. It can be any sort of tree; I have chosen a delicate and intricate one, with individually molded leaves.

For this project, you will need:

- *2 cups flour made into dough (see page 11)*
- *Wooden skewer or toothpick*
- *Small blossom cutter (optional)*
- *Small scissors*
- *Large paper clip*
- *Paint*
- *Varnish*

1 Make the trunk of the tree and the crown following the instructions for the Apple Tree project (page 80). Add a dough flowerpot and cover the crown with small molded leaves as for the bay tree.

3 Finally, add the bird. He is made from a small piece of dough, pointed at each end for the beak and tail, with his wings snipped with scissors as shown. Mark an eye with a skewer or toothpick.

2 Instead of apples, add small pears among the leaves. A few little bits of white blossom dotted between the fruit are very attractive and make the tree a little more interesting. If you do not have a small cutter, such as the type used in cake decorating, you can substitute tiny, molded daisy-like flowers (see Basic Techniques).

4 Add a large paper clip for hanging. Bake, paint as desired, and varnish as instructed in Basic Techniques.

WHEAT SHEAF WITH MOUSE

This original project was inspired by the wonderful harvest-time decorations seen at Thanksgiving. The wheat sheaf can be made in any size, from a dinky little 3 inches (76mm) to the largest your oven will hold.

To make a large sheaf, you will need:

- *2 cups flour made into dough (see page 11)*
- *Small sharp scissors*
- *Wooden skewer or toothpick*
- *Giant paper clip*
- *Varnish*

1 Roll half the dough ¼ inch (6mm) thick, and, using the template on page 120, cut out the basic keyhole shape required for the base of the sheaf. Dampen the bottom half of the base from the dotted line (on template) down, and then roll out long straws of dough. Lay the straws side by side across the base as shown in the diagram. Build up two layers of straws in this way.

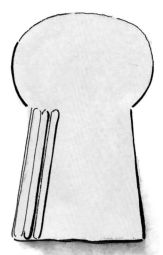

2 For heads of wheat, roll small cigar shapes approximately 2½ inches (64mm) long and ¾ inch (19mm) wide, and place them in overlapping rows all around the curved top edge of the keyhole shape, as shown in the diagram. Make sure that the final row covers the top end of the straws.

3 When all the stalks of wheat are in place, snip all the tops with small pointed scissors, as instructed in Basic Techniques (page 21).

4 Finally, add a small mouse (see page 26) to the stalks.

5 Push a giant paper clip into the top of your wheatsheaf. Bake and varnish as instructed in Basic Techniques and when it is dry, tie the sheaf with a ribbon.

6
FRUIT AND FLOWERS

FRUIT CLUSTERS

A bowl of dough fruits is a lovely alternative to wooden or plastic ones. They can be made life-size or smaller, like the ones used in the projects, following the instructions in Basic Techniques. If you make large individual fruits, bake them more slowly, as they will need a very long time to dry right through to the center and have a tendency to split if cooked too quickly.

This project is an alternative to individual fruits, and has different fruit clustered together on a base of leaves to make an attractive wall-hanging.

To make a fruit cluster, you will need:

- *1 cup of flour made into dough (see page 11)*
- *Cloves*
- *Wooden skewer or toothpick*
- *Large paper clip*
- *Paint*
- *Varnish*

I Make a roughly circular base from a flattened ball of dough and attach leaves all around the edge as shown. Make sure you leave a suitable place at the top for pushing in the paper clip.

2 Place an apple, orange, and pear, with a group of three strawberries and three plums at either side of the cluster. Add a strawberry flower and fill in the center with berries.

3 Push a large paper clip into the top for hanging, then bake, paint, and varnish as instructed in Basic Techniques.

POT OF PANSIES

This unusual project, painted in really vibrant colors, makes a stunning decoration – wonderful for brightening up a winter windowsill.

To make this project, you will need:

- *2 cups flour made into dough (see page 11)*
- *Wooden skewer or toothpick*
- *Knife*
- *Giant paper clip*
- *Paint*
- *Varnish*

1 Roll out half the dough to ¼-inch (6mm) thickness, and, using the template on page 123, cut out the basic shape. Reroll the trimmings and cut out a second pot using the lower section of the template. Place it on top of the lower half of the basic shape so that it forms a double layer for the flowerpot part of this project. Lay a 1-inch (25mm) wide strip of dough across the top to form the lip of the pot.

3 Make ten pansies according to the instructions in Basic Techniques (page 17) and arrange a row of four across the center, then three each above and below. Finally, tuck a few extra leaves in between the flowers.

2 Make and place molded leaves, with the edges drawn up to form jagged edges, all the way around the top half of the basic shape, with one or two overlapping onto the pot, as shown in the diagram above.

4 Push a giant paper clip for hanging into the top of the flowers. Bake slowly, as the smooth pot part of this decoration has a tendency to rise and bubble if it is cooked too quickly. Paint as desired and varnish as instructed in Basic Techniques.

VASE OF ROSES

*B*oth this and the Jug of Mixed Flowers (overleaf) are variations on the Pot of Pansies (previous project), using different flowers and containers.

For this project you will need:
- *2 cups flour made into dough (see page 11)*
- *Wooden skewer or toothpick*
- *Giant paper clip*
- *Paint*
- *Varnish*

1 Roll out half the dough ¼ inch (6mm) thick and, using the template on page 124, cut out the basic shape. Cut another rolled-out piece of dough to the shape of the vase and, after dampening the base, lay this over the vase section so that it forms a double layer.

3 Fill in the top with a mass of roses (see Creating Basic Shapes, page 17), mostly full-blown, with a few buds tucked in the spaces. Tuck a few leaves in between the roses.

2 Make and lay leaves all around the top, with one or two overlapping onto the vase.

4 Add a giant paper clip for hanging and bake slowly, as the smooth area of the vase has a tendency to rise and bubble if it is cooked too quickly. Paint as desired and varnish as instructed in Basic Techniques.

JUG OF MIXED FLOWERS

This colorful pitcher of flowers gives you a chance to use your own imagination. By combining several of the techniques already learned in previous projects, you can produce a truly original piece of work.

To make a large jug of flowers, you will need:

- *2 cups flour made into dough (see page 11)*
- *Wooden skewer or toothpick*
- *Knife*
- *Giant paper clip*
- *Paint*
- *Varnish*

1 Roll out half your dough to ¼-inch (6mm) thickness and, using the template on page 125, cut out the whole shape. Using the same technique as in the Pot of Pansies (page 90), cut another jug and lay it on top of the base. Roll out a sausage of dough approximately 6 inches (152mm) long and attach it with a little water to the side of the jug to form the handle, as shown.

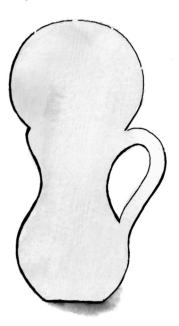

3 Push a giant paper clip into the top of your flowers, estimating the center of gravity so the model hangs straight. Bake slowly to keep the dough from rising, paint in colors of your choice, and varnish as instructed in Basic Techniques.

2 Make leaves of your choice and lay them all around the top, with a few overlapping onto the jug. Add a profusion of different flowers of your choice to make a lovely summer bouquet. You could make the flowers as instructed in Basic Techniques (page 17), but if you feel like being a little more adventurous, design a few new ones of your own. You can also experiment with making some of them from a side view, or in different stages of bloom.

7
WALL
SCULPTURES

WOODLAND SCENE

*A*mazingly, if you take a piece of wood, wet it, arrange some dough on top, and bake it in the oven, the dough sticks fast to the wood. There are many ideas that take advantage of this property of salt dough, such as using a wooden spoon as your base and adding face and hair to make a puppet. For this project, however, we use a precut slice from a tree trunk, readily available from florists. Make sure you buy one that has not been varnished.

To make the woodland scene, you will need:
- *1 cup flour made into dough (see page 11)*
- *Wooden base*
- *Wooden skewer or toothpick*
- *Small scissors*
- *Black-headed pushpin*
- *2 picture eyes*
- *Varnish*

1 Using your wooden base instead of a baking sheet, first form a tree in the top half of the piece of wood, following the instructions for the Apple Tree in Chapter 5 (see page 80).

2 At the base of the tree, add some extruded dough grass, a porcupine (see page 26), and a few leaves.

3 Bake and varnish as instructed in Basic Techniques. Once the varnish is dry, screw two picture eyes into the back of the wooden plaque and thread wire through them to hang your project on the wall.

This project can be varied in many ways; use your wooden base in the landscape (horizontal) rather than portrait (vertical) position, or paint all or part of the dough model. You can of course use a wooden base for other projects as well. Dough sculptures make particularly good name plates, although they are not suitable for outdoor use.

THATCHED COTTAGE

*T*his is another project which lends itself to a little improvisation. You could work according to the basic directions, or have fun changing details to suit yourself. For example, why not change the position of windows and doors or paint the model in different colors? Or why not model your own house in dough?

To make a thatched cottage, you will need:

- *2 cups flour made into dough (see page 11)*
- *Knife*
- *Potato ricer (preferably) or garlic press*
- *Wooden skewer or toothpick*
- *Large paper clip*
- *Paint*
- *Varnish*

1 Using the template on page 123, cut the shape for the cottage from dough rolled out ¼ inch (6mm) thick. Add a door frame made from thin strips of dough, and then mark the wooden planks of the door within the frame with a knife. Add window frames in the same way.

2 Construct the roof overhang above one of the windows from thinly rolled dough, supported on a sausage of dough placed just above the window frame. Cover the roof, except for the chimney, in thatch made from extruded dough, adding an attractively shaped ridge cut from thinly rolled-out dough at the top. Add lines to chimney to simulate brick.

3 Place flowers around the door, and leaves and grass along the base of the house.

4 Push a large paper clip into the top, calculating the center of gravity. Bake, paint as desired, and varnish as instructed in Basic Techniques.

Overhang

HATS

These pretty wall hangings can be made in a variety of sizes, with different colored ribbons and types of flowers.

To make a medium-sized hat, you will need:

- *1 cup flour made into dough (see page 11)*
- *Saucer*
- *Fork*
- *Wooden skewer or toothpick*
- *Small paper clip*
- *Paint*
- *Varnish*

1 Roll a ball of dough the size of a walnut and place it on your baking sheet. Roll out the remainder of your dough ¼ inch (6mm) thick and, using a saucer as your guide, cut a circle. Mark the edge of the circle all the way around with the prongs of a fork for a fancy edge. Lay the circle centrally over the ball of dough on your baking sheet.

2 For the ribbon, roll out a long, thin strip of dough approximately ½ inch (13mm) wide and 12 inches (305mm) long. Lay it around the crown of the hat and form a bow as shown in the diagram.

3 Make and place three small leaves and a flower over the center of the bow.

4 Make three small sausage-shaped pieces of dough and tuck them under the brim of the hat – one at the top and the other two at each side, to create a wavy effect in the brim.

5 Push a small paper clip into the support at the top of the brim. Bake, paint the ribbon and flowers, and varnish as instructed in Basic Techniques.

THE FOUR SEASONS

This set of small wall sculptures depicts the four seasons, but the idea can be adapted to any image. For example, a set of four sculptures could show different flowers or animals.

To make four small sculptures, you will need:

- *3 cups flour made into dough (see page 11)*
- *Saucer*
- *Wooden skewer or toothpick*
- *Potato ricer (preferably) or garlic press*
- *Small scissors*
- *4 large paper clips*
- *Paint*
- *Varnish*

Spring

Summer

1 Roll out your dough approximately ¼ inch (13mm) thick and, using a saucer as a template, cut four circles. The spring scene has a rabbit among some daffodils. Following the instructions in Basic Techniques for the daffodils (page 17), and Chapter 2 for the rabbit (see pages 36–37), build up your picture. Add some extra leaves around the flowers and some extruded dough grass at the bottom.

2 The summer scene is a beautiful bouquet of roses. Following the instructions in Basic Techniques (page 17), place a group of full-blown roses centrally on the sculpture. Fill in between them with buds and leaves, and tuck leaves underneath the roses around the perimeter.

Fall

Winter

3 The fall sculpture is constructed like spring, but with wheat and mice in place of the daffodils and rabbit. Following the instructions in Chapter 2, make two small mice (see page 26) and place them at the base of your sculpture. Roll out some long, thin stalks for the wheat and place them running up the right-hand side of your sculpture. Make a few cigar-shaped heads of wheat and, having snipped them with sharp scissors, place them at the tops of the stalks. Add a little extruded dough grass around the base of the sculpture.

4 The winter scene shows a traditional snowman. He is easily constructed from two balls of dough for the head and body, with the usual additions of hat, scarf, buttons, and carrot nose. Mark the eyes with a wooden skewer or toothpick. A piece of flattened dough at the base makes the snow-covered ground, and small dots of dough the falling snow.

5 Push a paper-clip hanger into the top of each sculpture. Bake, paint as desired, and varnish.

HARVESTTIME

This piece was inspired by a sketch in our church magazine at harvesttime. The abundance of fruit, vegetables, and bread give this project a real "fruits of the earth" appeal.

To make the harvest sculpture, you will need:

- *2 cups flour made into dough (see page 11)*
- *Cloves*
- *Small scissors*
- *Wooden skewer or toothpick*
- *Giant paper clip*
- *Paint*
- *Varnish*

1 Roll out half your dough to approximately ½-inch (13mm) thickness and, using the template on page 126, cut out an oval shape. Make and place a small basket slightly left of center on the sculpture base and fill with an assortment of small vegetables of your choice, made according to the instructions in Basic Techniques (page 18).

3 Arrange a bunch of wheat, made in the same way as in the Wheat Sheaf project, with the stalks running up the right-hand side of the sculpture and the heads curling around the top.

2 Around the base of the basket, arrange a group of bread and rolls and individual fruits, made according to the instructions in Basic Techniques.

4 Add a giant paper clip pushed into the top. Bake, paint, and varnish as instructed in Basic Techniques.

This and the following four sculptures are constructed as a variation on the same theme, thus providing a matching set should you want to make a collection.

This charming rooster is not as difficult to construct as it looks, and once you have mastered the art of producing the basic scene, you can put any farm animal you fancy into the field.

A word of warning: Large, heavy pieces of dough such as these are more susceptible than smaller pieces to stresses in the dough and are more inclined to crack (see Troubleshooting). This can be especially heartbreaking when you have spent time constructing your piece, so it is worth taking every precaution to prevent it from happening. Using a laminated dough (how-to instructions follow), as well as cooking your

dough at a lower temperature (maximum 225°F) for a longer period, should help prevent cracks. This may take up to 48 hours, after which you should cool it slowly by gradually reducing the oven temperature. Once you have switched the oven off, leave the sculpture in the oven to cool completely.

For the rooster sculpture, you will need:

- *3 cups flour made into dough (see page 11)*
- *Piece of nylon net 10 inches (250mm) square*
- *Knife*
- *Wooden skewer or toothpick*
- *Clove*
- *Potato ricer (preferably) or garlic press*
- *Giant paper clip*
- *Paint*
- *Varnish*

1 To laminate dough, first cut the net to the shape of the plaque, using the template on page 126. Roll out half the dough into a long, oval shape approximately 10 × 20 inches (508 × 254mm) and ¼ inch (6mm) thick. Brush the dough with water and lay the net on the upper half as shown. Fold up the lower half of the dough so it rests on top of the netting. Reroll the two layers together to make sure that the net is well embedded. The base should be about ⅜ inch (10mm) thick. This laminating process helps to prevent cracking once the dough is cooked.

2 Using the template again, cut your laminated sculpture to the required shape and size with a sharp knife, trying to keep the template centered over the net. Any bits of net left protruding from the edges can be cut off with scissors after cooking. Transfer to a baking sheet and moisten the surface with a little water. Add the fence, formed from flattened snakes of dough, across the center of the base in a slightly curved line. Place four fence posts made in the same way on top.

(Continued on page 110)

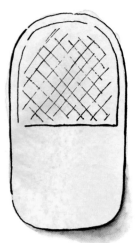

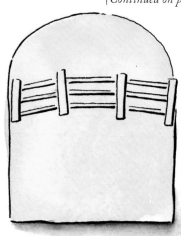

3 Add the tree next. Form the trunk as shown in Basic Techniques and place it between the two central fence posts. Add pinched dough leaves and small balls of dough for apples. It is a good idea to add a paper clip at center top at this stage; if it pushes the dough out of shape, a few more leaves on the tree will disguise this.

You now have your basic scene, ready to add the animals of your choice – in this case, a rooster.

4 To make the rooster, first form the head and body all in one piece from a smoothly rolled piece of dough the size of an orange. Form the dough into an elongated shape and gently narrow one end for the head, then flatten and bend the dough into shape as shown. Lay on the base over the foot of the tree trunk.

5 Add an elongated wing made from a flattened cone of dough marked with a paper clip. Form a small beak between thumb and index finger and attach to the head with a little water. The comb is cut with scissors from a flattened ball of dough and then attached to the top of the head. Small,

flattened teardrop-shaped pieces of dough are added just below the center of this for the eye, and below the beak for the crop.

6 The magnificent tail is made by hand-rolling lots of dough "worms" of different lengths, and piling them on top of each other. The legs are thinly rolled pieces of dough placed just under the body. Mark faint lines gently across the legs with a sharp knife. Claws are carefully molded from tiny pieces of dough and added to the foot of the raised leg.

7 The piece is finished by adding grass made from dough extruded through a garlic press or potato ricer along the bottom edge of the sculpture. Add a few leaves and flowers.

8 Bake as instructed on page 108. The painting of the comb in a vibrant red and the electric blue of the tail add to its attraction. Varnish as instructed in Basic Techniques.

*T*his second piece in the set of sculptures is constructed as for the previous project, but it is simpler to make. Ducks are a favorite with many people and are charming subjects for sculpture (see page 2).

For the duck sculpture, you will need:

- *3 cups flour made into dough (see page 11)*
- *Piece of nylon net 10 inches (254mm) square*
- *Knife*
- *Wooden skewer or toothpick*
- *Cloves*
- *Potato ricer (preferably) or garlic press*
- *Giant paper clip*
- *Paint*
- *Varnish*

1 Follow steps 1, 2, and 3, as for the Barnyard Rooster.

2 Add the first duck by placing a flattened piece of dough against the tree in the center. Make the head and beak as instructed for the ducks in Chapter 2 (see page 30).

3 Add the other two ducks as shown in the diagram, constructing them as shown in Chapter 2 (see page 30). Place bows at their necks and tuck feet under their bodies.

4 Add extruded dough grass at the bottom of the sculpture and a few leaves and flowers to fill in the spaces at the side.

5 Bake as instructed for the Barnyard Rooster, paint as desired, and varnish as instructed in Basic Techniques.

PIGS IN THE PEN

*G*loucester Old Spot pigs snuffling around in an orchard make a charming, old-fashioned rural scene, with the style of the pigs adding a comic touch.

For the pig sculpture, you will need:

- *3 cups flour made into dough (see page 11)*
- *Piece of nylon net 10 inches (254mm) square*
- *Knife*
- *Wooden skewer or toothpick*
- *Potato ricer (preferably) or garlic press*
- *Giant paper clip*
- *Paint*
- *Varnish*

1 Follow steps 1, 2, and 3, as for the Barnyard Rooster.

2 Once you have the basic scene consisting of field, fence, and tree, simply fill the field with pigs. You can add a mother pig with piglets, and individual pigs shown from both front and side views, as in the photograph. Instructions for pigs can be found in Chapter 2 (see page 32) – just make them a little smaller so that they will be in scale with the field.

3 Dot a few leaves and daisies (see Basic Techniques) between the pigs in the field, and add extruded dough grass in small clumps around the flowers and along the bottom edge of the sculpture.

4 Bake as instructed for the Barnyard Rooster, paint as desired, and varnish as instructed in Basic Techniques.

TENDING SHEEP

*T*his rather more complicated variation of the farm sculpture was inspired by a beautiful terra-cotta wall hanging on display in a friend's kitchen.

For the sheep sculpture, you will need:

- *3 cups flour made into dough (see page 11)*
- *Piece of nylon net 10 inches (254mm) square*
- *Knife*
- *Wooden skewer or toothpick*
- *Potato ricer (preferably) or garlic press*
- *Giant paper clip*
- *Paint*
- *Varnish*

1 Follow steps 1, 2, and 3, as for the Barnyard Rooster.

2 Once you have the fence and tree in place, add the shepherd. Working from the top down, make the crown of the hat first and then attach a brim to it. Place a small ball of dough below the hat for the head and, using the wooden skewer, mark in the hair and features. Don't worry too much about accuracy – just get the general impression of a face.

3 Tuck one small sausage-shaped arm underneath a triangular-shaped smock, and place the other arm on top, making creases in the smock fabric with the skewer. Add a piece of broken wooden skewer for his crook, and then position small balls of dough for hands. Finally, add a scarf around his neck.

4 Make several fat sausage shapes for the sheep's bodies and arrange them around the shepherd. Next, add heads to all the sheep, facing them in different directions, with ears on each head.

5 Mark the sheep's wool with the blunt end of a wooden skewer, and mark eyes and noses with the pointed end. Place extruded dough grass along the base of the sculpture.

6 Bake according to the directions for the Barnyard Rooster. Paint as desired and varnish as instructed in Basic Techniques.

A Cow and Two Geese

*I*nspiration for this scene came from an illustration of a farm in the Yorkshire Dales. You can almost imagine the cow beneath the trees to be part of the farmer's family!

For this project, you will need:

- *3 cups flour made into dough (see page 11)*
- *Piece of nylon net 10 inches (254mm) square*
- *Knife*
- *Wooden skewer or toothpick*
- *Potato ricer (preferably) or garlic press*
- *Giant paper clip*
- *Paint*
- *Varnish*

1 Follow steps 1, 2, and 3, as for the Barnyard Rooster.

2 Add a cow to your field, following the instructions in Chapter 2 (see page 40), but make your cow smaller so that it is in scale with its surroundings.

Shape for Geese

3 Make two geese by rolling out two pieces of dough to the shape shown in the diagram, bending the necks up. Add wings, beaks, and feet as shown.

4 Dot a few leaves, daisies, and tufts of grass around and between the animals, and add extruded dough grass along the base of the sculpture.

5 Bake according to the instructions for the Barnyard Rooster, paint as desired, and varnish as instructed in Basic Techniques.

Templates

hese templates are for specific projects and are actual size. To use, simply trace or photocopy the template onto thin cardboard. Cut out the shape, lay gently on top of the rolled-out dough, and cut around the outline using a sharp knife.

The templates may also be used to enlarge or reduce designs. In this case, the template will need to be enlarged or reduced using a photocopier. Remember, of course, that dough requirements will also vary with the size of the particular model.

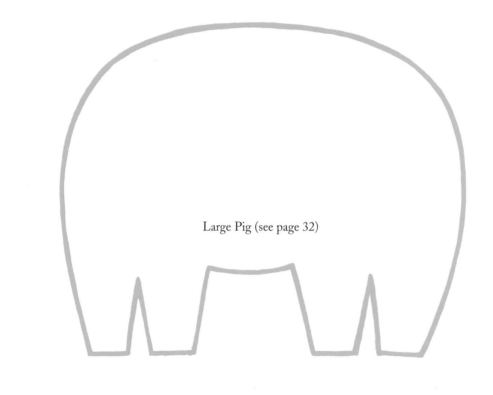

Large Pig (see page 32)

Mother Pig with Piglets (see page 33)

Small Pig (see page 32)

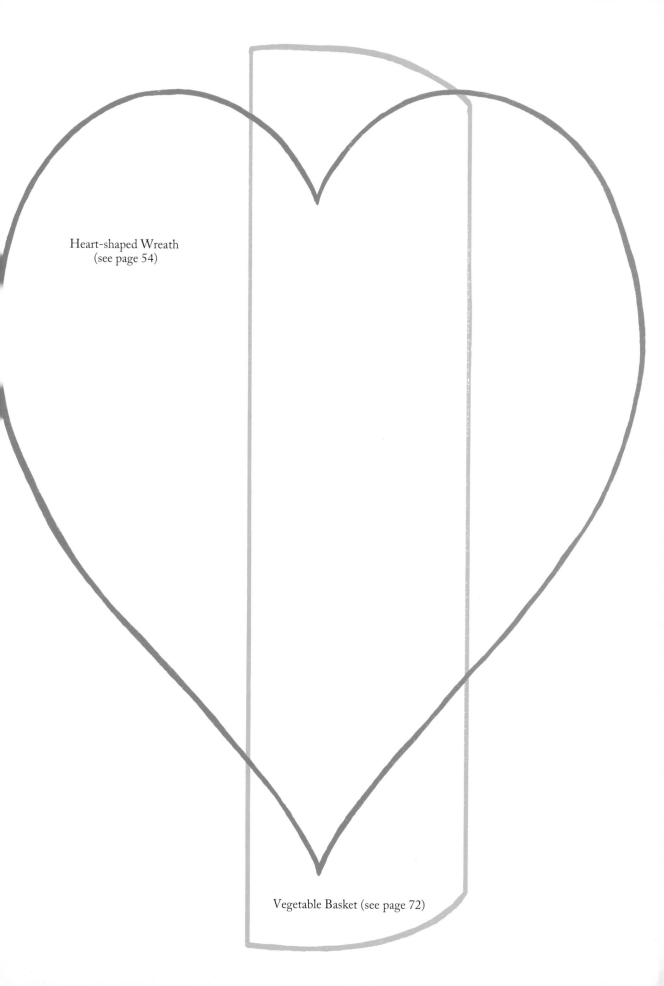

Heart-shaped Wreath
(see page 54)

Vegetable Basket (see page 72)

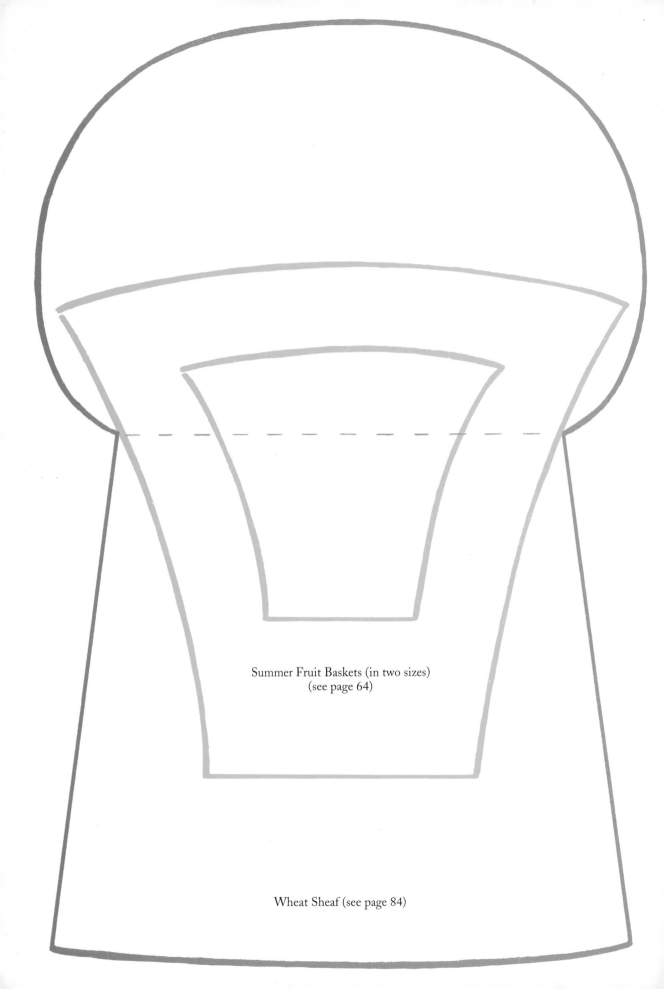

Summer Fruit Baskets (in two sizes)
(see page 64)

Wheat Sheaf (see page 84)

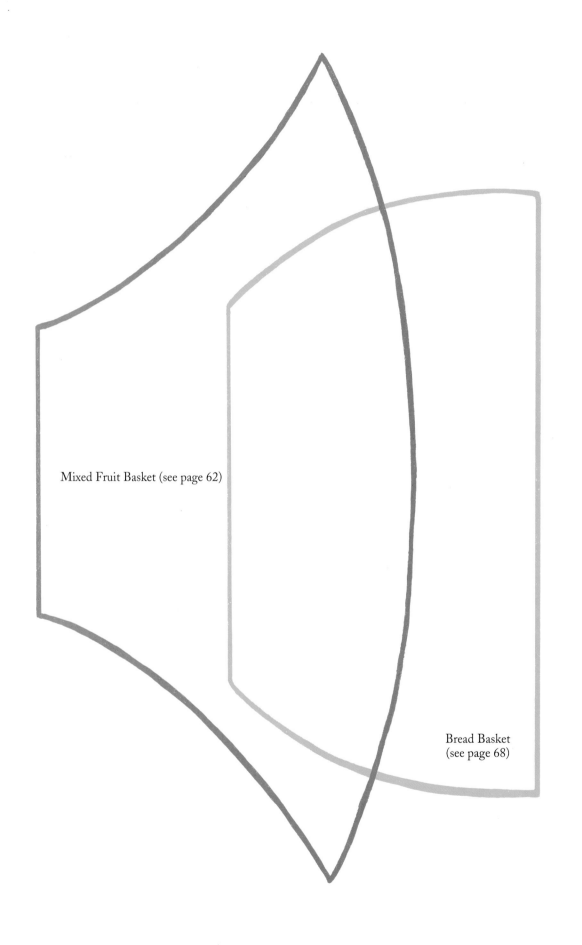

Mixed Fruit Basket (see page 62)

Bread Basket
(see page 68)

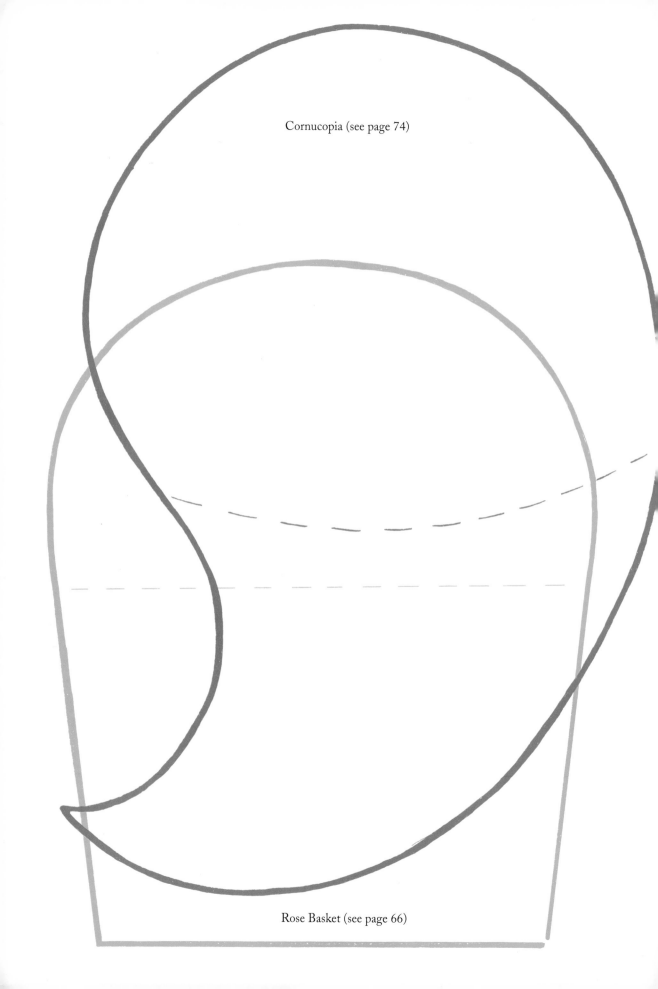

Cornucopia (see page 74)

Rose Basket (see page 66)

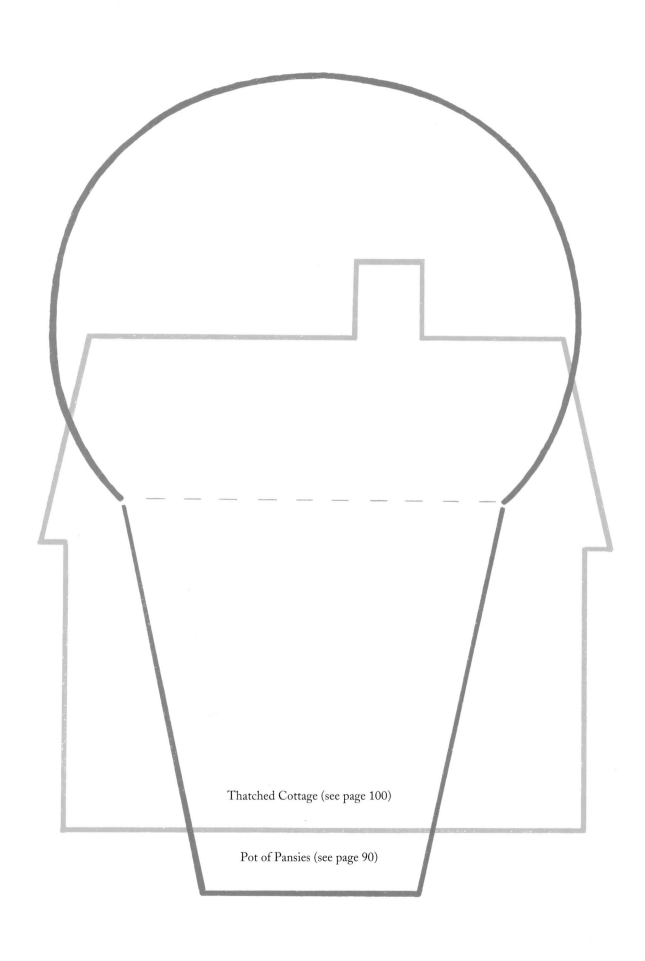

Thatched Cottage (see page 100)

Pot of Pansies (see page 90)

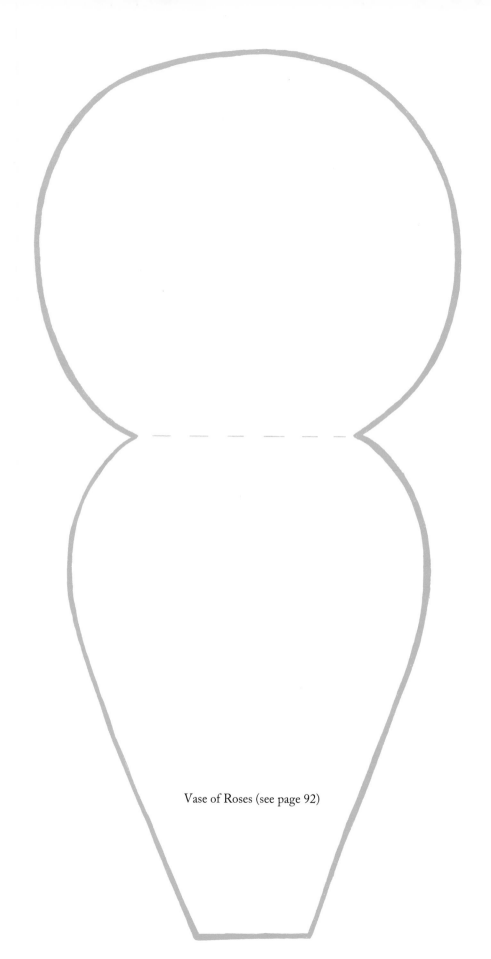

Vase of Roses (see page 92)

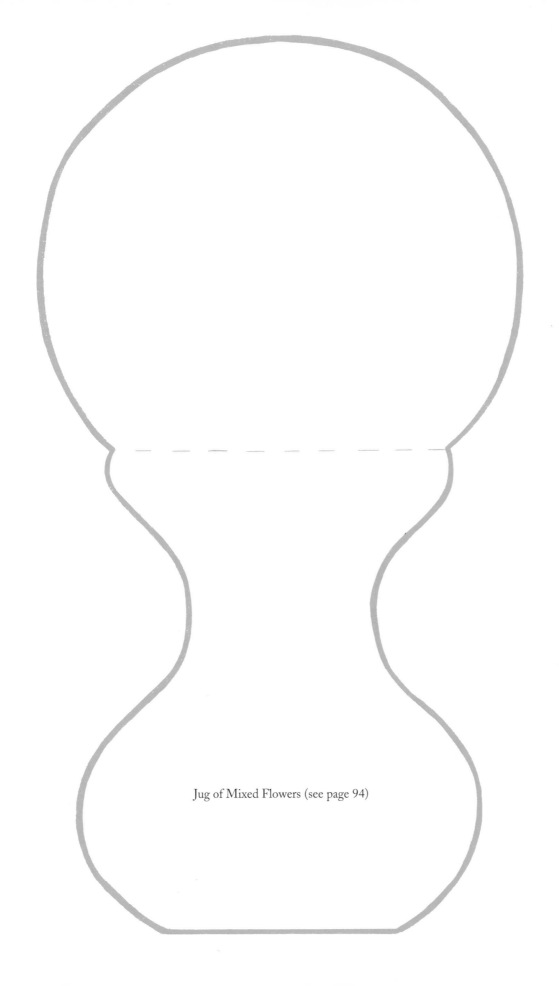

Jug of Mixed Flowers (see page 94)

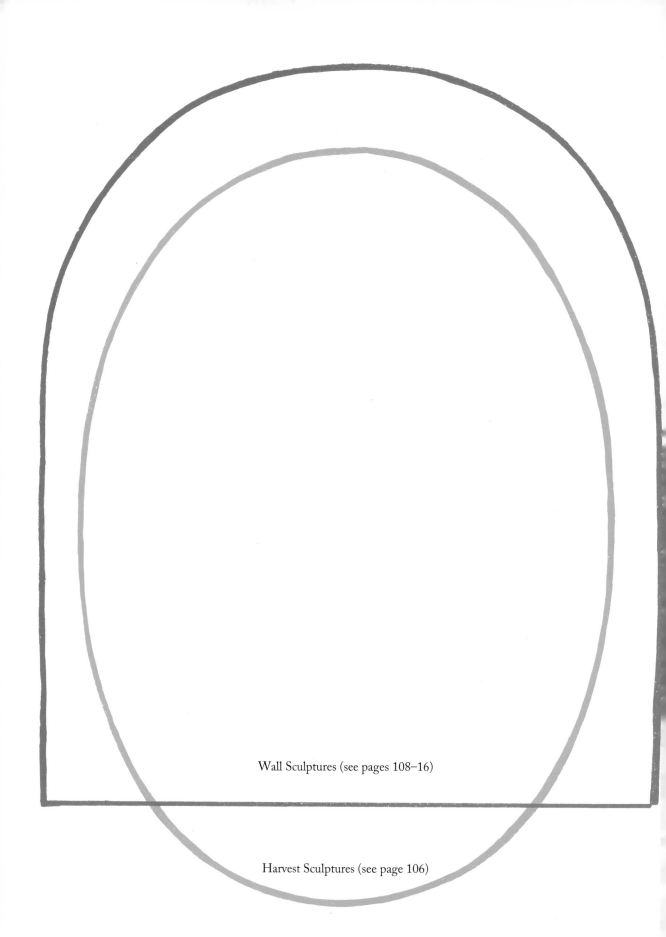

Wall Sculptures (see pages 108–16)

Harvest Sculptures (see page 106)